1982

LA FONTAINE
Poet and Counterpoet

LA FONTAINE
Poet and Counterpoet

MARGARET GUITON

RUTGERS UNIVERSITY PRESS
New Brunswick   *New Jersey*

Library of Congress Catalogue Card Number: 60-14205

Manufactured in the United States of America by
Quinn & Boden Company, Inc., Rahway, New Jersey

Contents

REREADING LA FONTAINE   vii

I   THE FOX AND THE CROW   2

II   THE FABLE: PROSE OR POETRY?   15
    The Fable Fiction
    The Fable Language
    The Fable Verse Form

III   THE FABLE AS COUNTERPOETRY   63
    The Poetic Comedy
    The Social Comedy
    The Human Comedy

IV   THE FABLE AS POETRY   125
    Words and Actions
    The Voice of Nature
    The Language of the Gods

V   A CITIZEN OF THE UNIVERSE   171

CHRONOLOGICAL TABLE   187

INDEX   191

Rereading La Fontaine

As the world becomes unfit for animal life, La Fontaine's fable world assumes, increasingly, the appearance of a privileged sanctuary. Were ever streams so limpid, grass so tender, or breezes so refreshing? It all seems a bit too good to be true and doubtless is.

One remembers that La Fontaine's earliest use of speaking animals, a salmon and a sturgeon, is in the allegory written to celebrate Fouquet's establishment at Vaux. The two fish, as he explains, were found in the Seine and brought to Fouquet, "who had them put in a very large, rectangular pool, where I found them, full of health and vigor, when I began my description [of Vaux]." This marriage of natural and artificial elements, the vigorous and healthy fish imprisoned in a "crystal palace," is characteristic of La Fontaine's fable poetry. Aesop's animals have been transported into a man-made environment, one of those idyllic gardens that abound in Renaissance art and poetry. To give an example, the motley delegation that sets off to pay tribute to Alexander—"quadrupeds, humans, elephants, earthworms, the bird republic," and one highborn lion—eventually reach a meadow (IV 12)

Tout bordé de ruisseaux, de fleurs tout diapré,
   Où maint mouton cherchait sa vie;
  Séjour du frais, véritable patrie
Des zéphyrs.

All bordered with streams, all dappled with flowers,
   Where many a sheep subsisted;
  Home of fresh breezes, true native land
Of the zephyrs.

The passage smacks strongly of Tasso and Ariosto, both favorites of La Fontaine. But the imaginary garden is inhabited by real animals, one of which happens to be a hungry lion.

Though the effect, as I have pointed out, is partially ironic the irony in no way weakens its appeal. Chinese artists similarly include real animals—and they are intensely real—in close-range landscape paintings to heighten the enchantment of the scene. To quote the author of a seventeenth-century painting manual:

> Fish must be painted swimming and darting with vitality. They should appear startled by a shadow, or they should be floating idly, opening and closing their mouths. As they float on the surface, dive, or glide through the water grass, the clear waters envelop them or ripple off them. Deep in one's heart one envies them their pleasure. . . .*

just as one envies the carp and the pike in La Fontaine's fable of the fastidious heron (VII 4):

> L'onde était transparente ainsi qu'aux plus beaux jours;
> Ma commère la carpe y faisait mille tours
>   Avec le brochet son compère.

> The water was transparent as on the finest days;
> My crony the carp was sporting there
>   With her crony the pike.

* Mai-mai Sze, *The Way of Chinese Painting*, Random House, 1959, p. 376.

One does not, on the other hand, envy the allegorical animals portrayed in Utopian systems like the Golden Age of classical antiquity or the Peaceable Kingdom prophesied by Isaiah:

> The wolf also shall dwell with the lamb, and the leopard shall lie down with the kid; and the calf and the young lion and the fatling together; and a little child shall lead them.
>
> And the cow and the bear shall feed; their young ones shall lie down together; and the lion shall eat straw like the ox.
>
> *Isaiah* 11:6-7.

Edward Hicks' numerous versions of the scene are instructive. While Indians and Quakers exchange fraternal greetings in the background, the animals depicted in the foreground stare out at us in mingled horror and incredulity. Which is the most pitiable of the wretched group? The indignant lion cub, nuzzled by calf and fatling,* who is being led by a diapered infant? The recumbent leopard, either drugged or in a state of shock? Or the lion, whose vacant, inward-turning gaze betokens sad memories of his former majesty? Even those who might be expected to welcome the new turn of events—the kid, the lamb, the ox—seem ill at ease, as though embarrassed to live on such intimate terms with their previous predators.

An uninformed observer might well infer that they had all been stricken by a dire calamity: one of those droughts that inhibit the normal impulses of animals so that they are able to foregather, unmolested, at the drinking hole; or a sickness which, as in La Fontaine's famous fable, has lowered their vitality (VII 1).

Ils ne mouraient pas tous, mais tous étaient frappés.
  On n'en voyait point d'occupés
A chercher le soutien d'une mourante vie;
  Nul mets n'excitait leur envie.

* Strange to say, given the context, a young animal fattened for slaughter.

Ni loups ni renards n'épiaient
La douce et l'innocente proie.
Les tourterelles se fuyaient;
Plus d'amour, partant plus de joie.

All did not die, but all were stricken.
   One saw none engaged
In seeking subsistence for a dying life;
   No food excited their appetite.
   Neither wolves nor foxes were on the watch
   For the gentle and innocent prey.
   The turtledoves avoided each other;
   No more love, and so no more joy.

Hicks' reformed predators—La Fontaine's plague is about the only way of expressing the all-too-human circumstance in animal terms—have actually been stricken with the same internal virus that previously divided man from the rest of created being and led to his fall from grace: the birth of consciousness, of conscience. Hence thought, hence art, hence civilization. Hence also doubt, anxiety, despair; hence loss of appetite; hence, worst of all, that devitalizing sense of *déjà vu*, monotony and pointlessness known as ennui, the "absolute ennui" that preyed on Baudelaire and which, in Valéry's words, "is in itself no more than naked life when it looks at itself clearly."

It is not surprising that poets, in whom awareness of life is raised to its highest power, should be particularly susceptible to this disease, often experienced as a lack of personal identity or being. They are fortunately equipped with a compensatory ability to enter into other forms of being. I am thinking not only of La Fontaine but also, since he comes nearer to the traditional conception of a poet, of Keats.

Where's the Poet? Show him! show him,
Muses nine! that I may know him!
'Tis the man who with a man
   Is an equal, be he King,
Or poorest of the beggar-clan,
   Or any other wondrous thing
A man may be twixt ape and Plato;
   'Tis the man who with a bird,
Wren, or Eagle, finds his way to
   All its instincts; he hath heard
The Lion's roaring, and can tell
   What his horny throat expresseth,
And to him the Tiger's yell
   Comes articulate and presseth
On his ear like mother-tongue.

This art of divination in which, for Keats as well as for La Fontaine, the art of poetry consists, is apparently based on a mimetic faculty. Keats' teacher, Cowden Clarke, remembered that, struck by a passage in Spenser they were reading together, Keats "*hoisted* himself up, and looked burly and dominant, as he said, 'what an image that is—*sea-shouldering whales!*' " Bates comments that the passage is characterized

by the sort of empathy—the adhesive, imaginative identification—that increasingly marked Keats' own poetry and that later deepened in his clairvoyant understanding of Shakespeare. The reaction Clarke remembers—the young apprentice entering into the image of the whales, feeling the weight on his own shoulders of the parting billows, and looking "burly" as he "hoisted himself up"—reminds us of another description, of Keats telling about a bear and instinctively imitating it, moving slowly about, with his paws dangling as he reared backward. One also thinks of Keats' puckish statement to his friend Richard Woodhouse, a few years later, that he could enter into a billiard ball as it rolled about, feeling "a sense of delight from its own roundness, smoothness, volubility, & the rapidity of its motion." *

"O to be a dragon," or whale, or billiard ball, or trout, or eagle! Is this not one of the principal virtues of metaphor? It permits us to incorporate, one might almost say to ingest, the vital energies and special aptitudes of other forms of existence: gives us the same enviable facility of motion in any element; the same intense delight in motion or repose; the same unthinking acceptance and enjoyment of the passing moment. The totems and rituals of savages which are intended to give men the special virtues of various animals are based on a similar sort of magic by association.

This is why the fable metaphor of the animal-man, purportedly designed to scold, more often pleases and entertains. As Keats observed: "What shocks the virtuous philosopher delights the c[h]ameleon Poet." La Fontaine's *Discours* to La Rochefoucauld (X 14) * points out that men are just as scatterbrained as rabbits. Scatterbrained or not, there are worse fates than dancing and banqueting upon the fragrant heath, at dusk or dawn, like the rabbits La Fontaine saw. Keats used a somewhat similar analogy in the long journal-letter to his brother and sister-in-law written in the spring of 1819. He begins by pointing out that men, himself included, are hardly more reasonable, or more disinterested, than animals.

The greater part of Men make their way with the same instinctiveness, the same unwandering eye from their purposes, the

* Walter Jackson Bates, *John Keats*, Oxford University Press, 1966, pp. 33-34.
* The same fable, three centuries before Konrad Lorenz, also describes the functioning of the territorial imperative—in dogs, statesmen, courtiers, coquettes, and authors.

same animal eagerness as the Hawk—The Hawk wants a Mate,
so does the Man—look at them both they set about it and
procure on[e] in the same manner. They want both a nest and
they both set about one in the same manner—they get their
food in the same manner— The noble animal Man for his
amusement smokes his pipe—the Hawk balances about the
Clouds—that is the only difference of their leisures. This it is
that makes the Amusement of Life—to a speculative Mind. I
go among the F[ie]lds and catch a glimpse of a stoat or a field-
mouse peeping out of the withered grass—the creature hath a
purpose and its eyes are bright with it. I go amongst the build-
ings of a city and I see a Man hurrying along—to what? The
Creature has a purpose and his eyes are bright with it.*

See how the simile, originally presented as a criticism of human
self-absorption, moves, almost automatically, in the opposite direction, pointing out the amusing, and even endearing, quality of
eager, unreflecting, busyness.

Keats then reverts to his original theme, regretting that the
"complete disinterestedness of Mind" exemplified by Socrates and
Jesus should be so rare. But he soon catches himself up, exactly
as La Fontaine might have done:

Even here though I myself am pursueing [sic] the same instinctive course as the veriest human animal you can think of . . . —
straining at particles of light in the midst of great darkness—
without knowing the bearing of any one assertion of any one
opinion. Yet may I not in this be free from sin? May there not
be superior beings amused with any graceful though instinctive
movement my mind m[a]y fall into, as I am entertained with
the alertnest [sic] of a Stoat or the anxiety of a Deer? Though
a quarrel in the streets is a thing to be hated, the energies dis-

* *The Selected Letters of John Keats*, Doubleday and Co., 1956, p. 242.

played in it are fine; the commonest Man shows a grace in his quarrel— By a superior being our reasoning[s] may take the same tone—though erroneous they may be fine— This is the very thing in which consists poetry; and if so it is not so fine a thing as philosophy— For the same reason that an eagle is not so fine a thing as a truth— *

La Fontaine, like Keats, and like the Virgil of the *Georgics*, considered poetry less fine a thing than truth, and his clearsighted recognition of this limitation, what I have called his "counter-poetry," saved him from the slipshod effusions of a lesser poet. The charm of natural existence, as represented in his fables, does not obscure its evils; but neither do these obvious evils obscure its charm. For present readers the latter insight is perhaps the more valuable of the two. Our truths are coming home to roost in plentiful abundance, each one more frightening than the one before. Eagles are rarer than they used to be.

* *Ibid.*, p. 243.

I

The Fox and the Crow

Le Corbeau et le Renard

Maître corbeau, sur un arbre perché,
  Tenait en son bec un fromage.
Maître renard, par l'odeur alléché,
  Lui tint à peu près ce langage:
  "Hé bonjour, Monsieur du Corbeau.
Que vous êtes joli! que vous me semblez beau!
  Sans mentir, si votre ramage
  Se rapporte à votre plumage,
Vous êtes le phénix des hôtes de ces bois."
A ces mots, le corbeau ne se sent pas de joie;
  Et pour montrer sa belle voix,
Il ouvre un large bec, laisse tomber sa proie.
Le renard s'en saisit, et dit: "Mon bon monsieur,
  Apprenez que tout flatteur
  Vit aux dépens de celui qui l'écoute.
Cette leçon vaut bien un fromage sans doute."
  Le corbeau honteux et confus,
Jura, mais un peu tard, qu'on ne l'y prendrait plus.

The Fox and the Crow

Master crow, perched on a tree,
  Was holding in his beak a cheese.
Master fox, enticed by the odor,
  Addressed him more or less in these terms:
    "Ah! good day, my dear Sir Crow.*
How pretty you are! how beautiful you seem!
  Truly, if your warbling
  Is in keeping with your plumage,
You are the phoenix of the denizens of this forest."
At these words, the crow is beside himself with joy;
  And to show his beautiful voice,
He opens a large beak, lets fall his prey.
The fox grabs it up, and says: "My good fellow,
    Learn that all flatterers
  Live off those who listen to them.
This lesson is well worth a cheese no doubt."
    The crow embarrassed and ashamed,
Swore, a bit too late, he wouldn't get caught again.

* I have not given a literal translation of the fox's opening line; the English language has no exact equivalent and I have tried to preserve the fox's tone. I am sure he would never have greeted the crow with five brusque monosyllables: "Ah! good day, Sir Crow."

Most of us learned, or read, the fable at a fairly tender age. How many of us were even faintly amused or pleased? How many of us actually realized that we were reading a poem? And how many of us have since reread and understood the poem as poetry? Has it not rather foundered among the irreclaimable bric-a-brac we carry with us through the years, like a familiar but useless household object? And yet the fable is a poem—a poem which, with its unexpected blend of humor and irony and sensuality, its harmonious and varied cadences, its virtuoso treatment of an unusual and complex verse form, demands a fairly discerning and experienced reader.

La Fontaine, who had little fondness for children, and still less for pedagogues, would have been surprised to learn that his fables would, to a large extent, survive as required school reading. He originally wrote them for a select elite of adult connoisseurs: the little coteries that gathered in the literary salons of his time. Madame de Sévigné, Madame de Lafayette, the Duc de La Rochefoucauld were among his admirers. So were a number of less reputable figures: the fascinating and amoral Duchesse de Bouillon, the libertine poet Saint-Evremond. Aesop's fables, then as now, were for children; but not the fables of La Fontaine. His choice of the familiar schoolroom genre merely gave added piquancy to a type of poetry so alien to the schoolroom atmosphere.

Our own childhood reading of the fable of the fox and the crow probably brought us little that we could not have found in Aesop: an anecdote and a moral. We have only to compare La Fontaine's fable with a more traditional version (here translated from the Greek by S. A. Handford) to realize how much we lost:

A crow sat in a tree holding in his beak a piece of meat that he had stolen. A fox which saw him determined to get the meat. It stood under the tree and began to tell the crow what a beautiful big bird he was. He ought to be the king of all the birds, the fox said; and he would undoubtedly have been made king, if only he had a voice as well. The crow was so anxious to prove that he *had* a voice, that he dropped the meat and croaked for all he was worth. Up ran the fox, snapped up the meat, and said to him: "If you added brains to all your other qualifications, you would make an ideal king."

The storyteller spells out, with somewhat laborious insistence, the underlying mechanics of his plot: the fox is flattering the crow because he is determined to get the meat; the crow is so anxious to prove that he *has* a voice that he drops the meat. We can hardly fail to get the point but we do not actually witness the event. We are not sure who the two animals are or why they are behaving as they do and, consequently, take little interest in their actions. La Fontaine, whose poem is not much longer than the prose fable, produces the opposite effect.

> Maître corbeau, sur un arbre perché,
> Tenait en son bec un fromage.
> Maître renard, par l'odeur alléché,
> Lui tint à peu près ce langage . . .

The curtain has risen on a drama, a form that can dispense with the obtrusive explanations of the author. We know, with the unreflecting certainty of an eyewitness, why the fox appears upon the scene and what he intends to do. Not *a* fox, as in the Aesopian fable, but "Maître renard," the particular fox that we are watching.

"Maître," a somewhat archaic term Rabelais often used for his animal heroes, changes color in its two contrasting contexts. As applied to the black-coated crow it acquires legal overtones— a connotation of bourgeois scholarship that will put the fox's subsequent "Monsieur *du* Corbeau" in proper perspective. As applied to the fox, it conveys a sense of expertise. The repetition of the word, in conjunction with La Fontaine's syntax, meter, and rhyme scheme, serves an important function. La Fontaine, no less concise and to the point than Aesop, uses the first two sentences of the fable to introduce the two fable characters. But the symmetrical treatment points up the underlying contrast and, such is the authority of poetic form, gives it a wider application. The "corbeau" (two syllables that impose a stupid open-mouthed expression on the face) and the "renard" (two syllables that are enunciated with a knowing half-smile) are here immortalized in an eternal antithesis of dupe and duper.

In substituting a cheese for the traditional piece of meat, La Fontaine is following the Latin poet, Phaedrus, who also put Aesop's fables into verse. The change is understandable. A piece of meat is not an attractive object, particularly when situated—shapeless, presumably raw—in the beak of a crow. If this is sufficient bait for Aesop's famished beast, how different do we feel ourselves to be! But Phaedrus's fox merely "sees" the crow with the piece of cheese. La Fontaine, whose fox is "enticed by the odor" of the cheese, develops the full potentialities of the transposition. The "fromage," here revealed as one of the most beautiful words in the French language, arouses the interest not only of that dainty epicure, La Fontaine's fox, but of the reader. "What kind of cheese?" one is almost moved to inquire. Is not the voluptuous "alléché" a sufficient indication? Certainly not an English cheddar or a round Dutch cheese. Perhaps a Camembert. Perhaps a Brie. The first four verses of the fable are impregnated by its delicate aroma: the tender *ge* and *che* sounds that linger at the rhyme in premonition of some delectable sensation.

The scene is now set for the fox's manipulation of the crow.

> "Hé bonjour, Monsieur du Corbeau.
> Que vous êtes joli! que vous me semblez beau!
> Sans mentir, si votre ramage
> Se rapporte à votre plumage,
> Vous êtes le phénix des hôtes de ces bois."

La Fontaine's fox has more or less disguised the straightforward logic of his Aesopian model. He approaches the crucial argument indirectly, though with amazing speed. In three short sentences he skyrockets from introductory courtesies, through the artless ejaculations of astonished admiration, to the noble figures of high-class literature. The two opening verses are calculated to catch the attention of the crow and convince him of the fox's sincerity. Why waste fine rhetoric on an indifferent or suspicious audience? The "ramage," which is distinctly literary, raises the tone a notch or two. It also reminds us that the fox, though engaged in his manipulation of the crow, still has his eyes riveted on the cheese. The tender, enticing syllable keeps rising to the surface, and very effectively. Had not the fox been working under some such stimulus, would he have ascended to the lyric heights of his concluding observations?

The first six verses of the fable consist of brief, factual, sharply punctuated phrases. "Sans mentir," the opening words of a particularly blatant lie, introduces a sustained and beautifully constructed period. Two octosyllables lead up to a twelve-syllable alexandrin,* the most powerful of all French verse forms and one that La Fontaine has reserved, intact, for this particular moment. (The earlier twelve-syllable verse, "Que vous êtes joli! que vous me semblez beau!" is too abrupt and discontinuous to have the unified sweep of a lyric alexandrin.) The ninth of eighteen verses, it is at once the center and the climax of the poem; and "phénix," which falls at the accented sixth syllable, or caesura, is the apex of the climactic verse. One might suppose that La Fontaine constructed the entire fable around this rich, exotic, and dramatically situated epithet. It was actually an inspired afterthought.

A number of delicate adjustments are involved. A literal translation of Aesop would have given: "Vous seriez le roi des hôtes

---

* I shall use this spelling to distinguish the French alexandrin from the very different English Alexandrine.

de ces bois" ("You would be the king of the denizens of this forest"). La Fontaine sometimes uses internal rhymes for their shock value, as in the ensuing verse. The "roi"-"bois" collision is exactly the reverse of what is needed here. One false move and the tenuous illusion will be torn apart. In addition, the brusque monosyllable "roi" at the caesura creates an unpleasant jerky movement that in and of itself is undesirable.

In his first version of the fable La Fontaine, apparently following Phaedrus's "nulla *prior* ales foret" ("no bird would excel you"), wrote: "Vous êtes le premier des hôtes de ces bois" ("You are the first of the denizens of this forest"). The two-syllable word at the caesura improves the rhythm of the alexandrin. Still, "premier" is too pale an epithet for the key word of the fox's speech; the expectorated *p* is inadvisable; the terminal *ier* is weak. La Fontaine needed two syllables that would carry the fable to its topmost peak. The perfect, the irreplaceable word at this particular moment is, and must be, the word "phénix"— not merely a royal but a supernatural bird and at the same time a poetic figure for a rare and almost supernatural type of excellence! It begins with a suave *ph*, which recalls the *f* of "fromage," and ends with an authoritative *ix*, which gives the alexandrin a strong and nobly rounded cadence. The fox—a sportive Molière marquis doffing his heavily plumed hat—is describing a sweeping Comédie-Française arabesque with his bushy tail.

What is both amusing and surprising is the total lack of preparation for this startling hyperbole. The fox, aware that pleasurable illusions are generally unaffected by the laws of common sense, does not even bother to give his flattery a veneer of plausibility. It is thus that Oronte addresses the Misanthrope in Molière's comedy:

> L'Etat n'a rien qui ne soit au-dessous
> Du mérite éclatant que l'on découvre en vous.

    The Nation has nothing that is not inferior
To the dazzling merit one finds in you.

The crow, unlike the Misanthrope, never senses the latent insult
to his intelligence:

A ces mots, le corbeau ne se sent pas de joie . . .

Another alexandrin, but a somewhat offbalance alexandrin
strongly accented on the third, sixth, and final syllables. The ex-
plosive internal rhyme, "A ces mots, le corbeau," in conjunction
with the terminal rhyme, which ties the verse to the preceding
verse, and the shift from a past to a present narrative tense,
creates an impression of almost instantaneous cause and effect.
Five short vowel sounds are propelled, with gathering speed,
toward the rich, triumphant "joie." Here, unmistakably, is the
first shuddering thrill of sudden self-realization—an emotion that
suggests the tremulous upward-straining attitude of a bird about
to break into song.

        Et pour montrer sa belle voix,
    Il ouvre un large bec, laisse tomber sa proie.

"*Sa* belle voix" versus "*un* large bec." Much is implied in La
Fontaine's rather unexpected use of these two innocent little
words. The crow is convinced he has a beautiful singing voice; he
is unaware he has so large a beak.
    Rousseau, though he considered the fable unethical, particu-
larly admired La Fontaine's description of the falling cheese.
"This verse is admirable, the harmony alone creates the image.
I see a big, ugly, open beak; I hear the cheese falling through the
branches." The effect depends on the general construction of the
poem. La Fontaine's fable, after reaching its highest altitude at
"phénix," coasts along on accumulated momentum until the

moment the crow opens his beak, when it stops short; then, like the cheese, it makes a vertical descent to earth. "Bec" is the cru-cial word, the turning point of the entire fable. A wide-open, gaping beak is an ugly spectacle, a shocking one if you have been previously admiring the plumage of a bird as La Fontaine's fox has more or less invited us to do. Baby birds, so charming in themselves, become hideous at meal time. "Bec," too, is an ugly word; in French ("*corbeau*," "*bec*"), a crowish word. The heavy monosyllable, here following a slow and somehow insidious pro-gression of sounds, falls into place at the caesura with the cool precision of a coin dropped into a slot. Out comes the cheese, and slithers through the branches to the ground.

Le renard s'en saisit, et dit: "Mon bon monsieur . . ."

The internal rhyme ("*saisit, et dit*") echoes the previous "mots"—"corbeau" in inverse order. The fox's first speech pro-duced the desired effect of making the crow drop the cheese. He is now about to make a moral commentary on the incident. His opening words, a familiar and somewhat patronizing "Mon bon monsieur," stand in apposition to the previous "Monsieur du Corbeau" and are a good indication of the fox's sudden shift of tone.

"Apprenez que tout flatteur
Vit aux dépens de celui qui l'écoute.
Cette leçon vaut bien un fromage sans doute."

I think this is the only time La Fontaine uses a seven-syllable verse in combination with a decasyllable and an alexandrin. The meter is so uncertain as to convey the quality of prose speech, a pointed, aphoristic prose. The so-desirable "fromage" of the open-ing verses seems almost commonplace now that the fox has brought it back to earth and is gulping it down in a succession of incisive, terminal *ts*. One last bite—"sans dou*te*"—in both literal and figurative senses, and he will be off to greener pastures. One can be sure he has enjoyed himself. To make a fool of someone and give him a moral lecture about it afterwards! And, wonder of wonders, the crow seems just as deeply affected by Master fox the moralist as by Master fox the poet.

> Le corbeau honteux et confus,
> Jura, mais un peu tard, qu'on ne l'y prendrait plus.

In other words, he all but apologizes for his previous credulity.

This is the very trick La Fontaine has simultaneously played upon his reader, even though the reader, unlike the crow, has the advantage of foreknowledge. We are well aware, before we even start the fable, that we are heading toward a moral: appearances are deceitful; don't believe everything you are told; don't speak with your mouth full. By the time we reach the moral we have succumbed entirely to the spell of La Fontaine's poetry and must be brutally awakened by the falling cheese.

La Fontaine's fable poetry, like all great lyric poetry, is a form of verbal seduction; but La Fontaine has added a further refinement to the familiar game. The reader is informed that he is being seduced, and on the flimsiest of all possible grounds: by certain words arranged in a certain order. Should he forget, and totally abandon himself to the illusion of poetry, La Fontaine is there to wake him up with a sudden change of tone, a broken meter, or a falling cheese. So perilous an equilibrium demands a reader who can keep his balance. We must remain as simple, as responsive as the crow, as flexible, as wary as the fox. Most poetry supposes "a willing suspension of disbelief." What Coleridge apparently considered a special concession of the poetry reader appeared to La Fontaine as the most natural, the most enjoyable, and the most precarious of mental postures.

II

The Fable: Prose or Poetry?

The Fable Fiction

Quand j'aurais, en naissant, reçu de Calliope
Les dons qu'à ses amants cette muse a promis,
Je les consacrerais aux mensonges d'Esope:
Le mensonge et les vers de tout temps sont amis.

Had I, at my birth, received from Calliope
The gifts that this muse has promised her lovers,
I would have consecrated them to the lies of Aesop:
Lies and verses have always been friends.

With these verses, which introduce his second book of fables,
La Fontaine, following the example of the Latin fable writer
Phaedrus (Fable 72), acknowledges and defies the traditional
adversary of his chosen fable form: the antithetical medium of
epic poetry. The antithesis would be less striking had the two
forms not an important common denominator. Together they
constitute the two fundamental human mythologies or, as La
Fontaine puts it, "lies": the fiction of man the demigod and the
fiction of man the animal. But whereas Calliope, the muse of
epic poetry, is, by extension, considered the muse of poetry in
any form, the fable has no muse or tutelary deity. In other words,
it is generally assumed that the heroic myth of man the demigod is essentially poetic, the fable myth of man the animal essentially prosaic.

The assumption no doubt corresponds to a common belief that it is the function of poetry to present an idealized, at least a magnified, version of ourselves—a belief that would seem more typical of Homeric Greece than of seventeenth-century Paris. But writers often inherit, and without too much reflection, the literary assumptions of their ancestors. The academician Patru, a respected literary authority of the time, did his best to persuade La Fontaine to write his fables in prose. Boileau omitted the fable from the inventory of legitimate poetic forms in his *Art poétique*, which appeared a few years after La Fontaine published his first volume of fables.

La Fontaine, when he points out the similarity of the epic and the fable, is thus clearly on the defensive. My choice of the fable, he implies, does not mean that I am lowering my poetic sights. Even if I were able to write a more ambitious type of poetry I would still prefer to write fables. Granted that these fables—"Aesop's lies"—are no more than transparent fictions, are they any worse than Homer's lies? Poetry of any kind is based on lies. The word "lie," which is unexpectedly strong, suggests less a defense of the fable than a criticism of heroic poetry, or any poetry—a rather unexpected criticism given La Fontaine's previous and continuing enthusiasm for the conventional fictions of poetry.

La Fontaine's original ambition—an ambition that was to haunt him all his life—was to revive the heroic style no longer fashionable in late seventeenth-century poetry. This is not to say that he attempted to emulate the virile grandeur generally associated with the idea of epic poetry (though, a self-styled disciple of Lucretius, he once ill-advisedly wrote a science epic on the remedial virtues of quinine). Technically speaking, the heroic style in La Fontaine's day merely demanded an action, generally taken from classical antiquity, involving some element of the supernatural. Two forms of heroic poetry were thus possible: the virile epic style of Homer and Virgil's *Aeneid*, suitable for celebrating the exploits of great heroes; the more flowery style of Virgil's *Eclogues* and Ovid's *Metamorphoses*, suitable for amorous scenes in rustic settings.

It was the second, lesser, style that La Fontaine had in mind. His first major poem was the heroic idyl *Adonis*, which he presented to the *Surintendant des Finances* Fouquet in 1658, thus earning the patronage of the richest and most generous Maecenas of the day. When the poem was first published in 1669, La Fontaine had already published his first volume of fables. He nonetheless insisted that he still preferred the heroic style to any other: "It is without doubt the most beautiful of all, the most rich, the most susceptible to ornaments and to those noble and audacious figures that make a special language, a language so charming as to deserve to be called the language of the gods."

Heroic poetry, for La Fontaine, is thus poetry in its party clothes, poetry that will give the greatest scope to his ambitions as a poet, poetry, in other words, that is confined to the realm of conventional make-believe. He never altogether abandoned the belief. Between 1659 and 1661 La Fontaine wrote his uncompleted *Songe de Vaux*, an allegory in celebration of Fouquet's new residence at Vaux-le-Vicomte. *Les Amours de Psyché et de Cupidon* a long prose narrative interspersed with occasional passages of poetry appeared in 1669; *La Captivité de Saint Malc* which, although based on a Christian theme, is treated in conventional pastoral style, in 1673. All these and, later, his unabashedly saccharine operas were to carry him further and further down the road of unreality—an unreality by then outmoded, which did not even have the saving grace of pleasing his immediate contemporaries.

La Fontaine's contes, produced in rapid succession from 1665 until the very end of his life, give a better picture of late seventeenth-century tastes in poetry. These stories in verse form, taken from Renaissance storytellers like Ariosto and Boccaccio, were extremely popular in La Fontaine's day. But the archly pseudoarchaic manner that La Fontaine developed for the conte now seems still more insipid than the faded gallantries of his heroic style.

The storytellers whom La Fontaine was imitating had had no compunction about calling a spade a spade and had described the manners and morals of their day with considerable zest and realism. This straightforward approach to sexuality was no longer possible in seventeenth-century France. It had given way to the blush and the leer and what Peter Quennel has called "that detestable ingredient, *le sel gaulois.*" No breath of Renaissance vitality survives in La Fontaine's stories. The main point was to suggest the by then unmentionable events or objects his predecessors had spelled out in black and white, to come as close as possible to outright indecency without actually saying the word and thus involve the reader in the complicity of the pointless but off-color anecdote.

As La Fontaine himself admitted, the conte was actually no more than a fashionable parlor game, and a game with fairly limited possibilities. In order to keep it going at all La Fontaine was gradually obliged to increase the ante, so, as volume followed volume, the suggestions became increasingly suggestive and the indecency increasingly indecent. Here again unreality, though unreality of a more highly seasoned flavor, seemed a necessary ingredient of pleasurable poetry.

And yet the great achievement of French literature in every other field during the 1660's and 1670's was that, although a highly social literature, sensitive in tone and style and manner to the atmosphere of the salon and the court, it nonetheless effected the vital contact with unvarnished human reality which, from that time on, has remained its central characteristic. Within a period of approximately twenty years Molière, Racine, Madame de Lafayette, and La Rochefoucauld dispelled the agreeable illusions so essential to fairy stories, polite society and power politics, so fatal to literature. The fairy story, having lost its foothold in the novel and the theater, was thenceforward restricted to the fairy story itself, which became a fashionable genre in the last years of the century; to operas, ballets—the whole royal pageant of Versailles; and to poetry.

As Boileau, the leading theorist of the day, observed in his *Art poétique*, poets must adhere strictly to the themes of classical mythology for the very reason that these themes are fictitious. Biblical themes are unsuitable because they introduce an incongruous element of reality into the illusion of poetry. Familiar names and objects are unsuitable for a similar reason, and Boileau criticizes Ronsard's habit of combining conventional poetic themes with the familiar facts of country life, recklessly changing "Lycidas into Jack and Phyllis into Jill." We here see the emergence of a point of view to be asserted still more emphatically by the Cartesian, Fontenelle, to attain the status of an established truth in the scientifically minded, rationalistic eighteenth century: poetry is no more than an agreeable fairy tale, a fairy tale so fragile as to be shattered by any contact with reality.

La Fontaine freely admitted that he too, like almost everyone, loved fairy stories—a taste apparent in much that he wrote. But, as he grew older, he tended more and more to view this taste as a typical human weakness, not a justifiable aesthetic attitude. It was his misfortune to be born a poet in an age that was particularly unpropitious for poetry. He was nonetheless aware of the powerful new stimulus at work in other fields. In fact this struck him at a fairly early moment in his career.

On the evening of August 17, 1661, Fouquet organized a magnificent fete at Vaux in honor of Louis XIV—a good deal too magnificent in the opinion of Louis XIV himself. Fouquet was soon afterward arrested for misuse of public funds and spent the rest of his life in prison. The dramatic anticlimax that so brutally revealed the sordid realities underlying the gay festivities was a lesson La Fontaine remembered all his life. On the night of the fete, however, he was completely unaware of these realities. His naïve enthusiasm for the spectacle overflows, five days later, in a letter to the poet Maucroix, another Fouquet protégé then absent on a mission in Rome: the beauty of the women, the delicacy of the food, the splendor of the decorations, the brilliance of the illuminations, the ingenuity of the theatrical machinery.

La Fontaine, later on in life, expressed a strong distaste for the complicated theatrical machinery that had become fashionable in late seventeenth-century ballets and operas. On the evening of the Vaux fete he was all astonished delight:

> On vit des rocs s'ouvrir, des termes se mouvoir,
> Et sur son piédestal tourner mainte figure.
> > Deux enchanteurs pleins de savoir
> > Firent tant par leur imposture,
> > Qu'on crut qu'ils avaient le pouvoir
> > De commander à la nature . . .

> One saw rocks open, caryatids move,
> And many a figure turn on its pedestal.
> > Two enchanters, rich in their lore,
> > Were so successful in their imposture,
> > That one believed they had the power
> > To dictate their commands to nature . . .

This elaborate bit of legerdemain was the prelude to Molière's new comedy, *Les Fâcheux*, then being performed for the first time. La Fontaine, for all his delight in the fairy-tale ballet, was quick to hail and make common cause with what he recognized as the new look in French comedy. "This is my man!" he exclaims, and then proceeds, with all the condescension of the inner-circle cognoscenti, to inform the absent Maucroix that "we" men of letters have changed our methods. The old-fashioned comedies we used to think so funny have become a thing of the past

Et maintenant il ne faut pas
Quitter la nature d'un pas.

And now one must not
Stray a single step from nature.

La Fontaine, as a result of the fete, was to lose a generous patron—a loss he must have bitterly regretted during the ten lean years that elapsed before Madame de La Sablière finally took him under her wing. He had discovered a new approach to literature. La Fontaine's use of the word "nature"—that bluntest instrument in the whole tool shop of literary theory—as the key slogan of this approach is not particularly enlightening. But one can make a rough distinction between the literary enchanters, who use their arts to create a more extravagant or a prettier universe, and the literary naturalists, who use their arts to illuminate some aspect of the existing universe. The La Fontaine of *Adonis, Le Songe de Vaux* and *Psyché* belongs, grosso modo, to the former category; the La Fontaine of the fables to the second. The La Fontaine of the fables is, however, concerned with certain aspects of the existing universe that are of little or no interest to his contemporaries.

The word "nature," as used by Molière, Racine, La Rochefoucauld, refers to one theme and to one theme only: the nature of the human animal. All the peripheral themes arising out of man's relation to the surrounding universe are ruled out of bounds as evading the possibilities of rational analysis. La Fontaine, in his fables, is also interested in the nature of the human animal. But, like Montaigne, like Pascal, he cannot consider the problem without placing it in its wider context—and in so doing he changes the basic character of the problem. "Nature," as used in La Fontaine's later fables, actually refers to the whole order of animate existence, a subject that can be known only through the type of imaginative sympathy that is a special proclivity of poets. The same fanciful and dreamy bent that so frequently tempted La Fontaine into the realm of make-believe plays an important role in his fables. Freed of the cumbersome trappings of literary convention, it becomes an approach to the great comedy, or drama, of natural existence which, as he informs us in the introduction to the fifth book of fables, was La Fontaine's chosen theme.

La Fontaine's collected fables cover a fairly extensive period of time. The first six books were published in 1668, seven through eleven in 1678 and 1679, and the twelfth book appeared in 1694. The earliest fables, which probably date back to the days at Vaux, preceded his various, and sometimes contradictory, theories of the fable form. La Fontaine liked to write fables and discovered, when he read them to his friends, that they were well received. This probably sufficed as far as La Fontaine was concerned. When the separate fables were assembled and published together in 1668, a theory, at least a justification of some sort, seemed necessary.

The Latin fable writer Phaedrus, whom La Fontaine sometimes follows in the early fables, had introduced his own collection with the following explanation:

The author Aesop discovered this material
That I have polished in six-foot verses.
The double portion of the little book: it makes us laugh
And teaches life by the warnings of the prudent man.
However, should anyone want to attack
My talking trees, still more wild animals,
Remember we are joking with fictitious fables.

This declaration of a serious moral aim sets Phaedrus's volume of collected fables in the general category of didactic poetry, a genre previously illustrated by Lucretius' *Of the Nature of Things* and Virgil's *Georgics*. As if to underline the parallel, Phaedrus, like Lucretius and Virgil, divided the volume into a number of separate books, each introduced by a dedication or a poem setting forth the general character and purpose of the work.

La Fontaine followed this example. His introductory dedication to the Dauphin, after a semi-ironic, semi-defiant allusion to the opening words of Virgil's *Aeneid*, restates the general argument set forth by Phaedrus:

> Je chante les héros dont Esope est le père,
> Troupe de qui l'histoire, encor que mensongère,
> Contient des vérités qui servent de leçons.

> I sing the heroes who were fathered by Aesop,
> A troop whose history, although mendacious,
> Contains truths which serve as lessons.

His volume is divided into six books and the introductory fables in Books II-VI open with dedications or explanatory passages describing the character and moral value of the fable.

La Fontaine's later fable poetry owes a good deal to Lucretius and to Virgil. But the suggested parallel, as here presented, is misleading. The moral gravity of Lucretius' and Virgil's didactic poetry stems from the poet's concern for factual truth. The moral principles of the fable, as Phaedrus and La Fontaine so readily admit, are founded on pure fiction; and the more explicitly these principles are stated, the more transparent the fiction shows itself to be.

The contradiction, of no particular concern to Aesop, is embarrassing for a poet, a point well illustrated in La Fontaine's preface to his first volume of fables. La Fontaine, intent on dignifying his chosen medium, points out that Plato's Socrates, though he banished Homer from his ideal Republic, spent the last days of his life putting Aesop's fables into verse. The anecdote supports La Fontaine's defence of the moral value of the fable; it completely undermines his defence of the fable as a poetic genre. Plato's Socrates considered poetry a dangerous stimulant, and the better the poetry the more dangerous the stimulant. He apparently tolerated the fable because the fable is so weak a fiction as to be innocuous, though useful as a simple, didactic form. As La Fontaine explains, the fable is divided into two parts: the anecdote, which is the body; the moral, which is the soul. The fictitious anecdote makes the moral truth more palatable but since fiction and truth are lodged in two incommunicable departments the one can never penetrate the other. The truth is uncorrupted by the fiction; the fiction makes no pretense of being true. This hard distinction between body and soul, or pleasure and utility, is exactly what had hitherto destroyed the underlying metaphor of the fable and prevented it from attaining the stature of poetry.

The fable metaphor, if we are to judge by its hold on the human imagination from primitive times until the present day, is a powerful one. But, whereas writers of epic poetry, following Homer, had consistently used the heroic myth of man the demigod as an expressive, or poetic, form, fable writers, following Aesop, had consistently used the fable myth of man the animal as an instrumental, or prosaic, form. In thus degenerating into a practical instrument, a brief anecdote intended to illustrate a moral truth, the fable metaphor was torn asunder, devitalized. The whole natural universe of the fable was reduced to a series of abstract symbols. The fox was sly, the ass stupid, the peacock vain, not through an imaginative use of language but by mere linguistic convention.

This is the common fate of familiar metaphors of any sort. Language, if it is to remain an expressive form, must be continually reactivated by poets, who either create new metaphors or else reanimate the dying metaphors. The latter problem, which is no doubt the more difficult of the two, was the real problem confronting La Fontaine when he decided to use the fable as a poetic form. And La Fontaine's perception and reanimation of the powerful metaphor underlying the barren symbolism, his effective incarnation of the invisible anatomy of the human mind in the concrete movements of animal existence—these are the true justification of his belief that the fable myth is as divine as any other.

One might add that the fable, as used by La Fontaine, would certainly have shared Homer's exile from the ideal Republic of Plato. In fact Plato's description of the uncivic imitative poet, who varies his harmonies and rhythms in accordance with his themes, applies very well to certain aspects of La Fontaine's fable poetry: "his entire art will consist in imitation of voice and gesture and there will be very little narration."

Yet La Fontaine's fable poetry is more than a purely imitative art: it expresses a certain vision of reality, a vision both comic and imaginative and, in either case, incompatible with the narrow, didactic moralism of the prosaic fable. Consider, for example, the familiar fable of the heron (VII 4):

Un jour sur ses longs pieds allait je ne sais où
Le héron au long bec emmanché d'un long cou.
    Il côtoyait une rivière.
L'onde était transparente ainsi qu'aux plus beaux jours;
Ma commère la carpe y faisait mille tours
    Avec le brochet son compère.

One day on his long legs ambled I don't know where
The heron with the long beak fitted into the long neck.
    He was skirting the edge of a river.
The water was transparent as on the finest days;
My crony the carp was sporting there
    With her crony the pike.

These introductory lines convey the intensely single vision of imaginative poetry: a heron? yes, but more than a heron. La Fontaine has somehow managed to change himself into the bird that he is watching, to reproduce in his own mind the hesitant, aimless saunter down the crystal stream of consciousness on a beautiful summer morning. And he is inviting the reader to follow his example: one would like to share so pleasurable a ramble. Then, suddenly, La Fontaine breaks the tone, the melody, the whole perspective he has established:

Le héron en eût fait aisément son profit . . .

The heron could easily have taken advantage of them . . .

La Fontaine, it would appear, has waked up and is now observing his heron from the outside, and with a certain degree of curiosity: why doesn't he eat the fish?

Progressing a little further to the heron's disdainful rejection of the available provender, we find that La Fontaine, by way of a joke, has turned the bird into a conscious gourmet:

"Du goujon? c'est bien là le dîner d'un héron!
J'ouvrirais pour si peu le bec! Aux dieux ne plaise!"

"Fish bait? What dinner is this for a heron!
I should open my beak for such scraps! God forbid!"

The heron and the man, inextricably fused in the opening verses, have been deliberately sundered. We are now plunged into the double vision of comedy, a point of view that prevents us from taking the eventual Aesopian advice—don't be too difficult—very much to heart.

These two points of view—the single vision of imaginative poetry and the double vision of comedy—are constantly displacing each other in La Fontaine's fables. The double vision of comedy arises out of our recognition of two different and contradictory aspects of an identical situation—a conflict between appearance and reality, promise and performance, what we are intended to see and what we, sometimes perversely, see for ourselves. It thus prevails when La Fontaine, as in the case of the fastidious heron, deliberately reveals the fictional aspect of the fable metaphor by endowing his characters with specifically human traits that belie their supposedly animal natures. The metaphor of the animal-man then operates on two levels. The animal-man thinks he is a man, or subject, the focal point of a universe expressly designed for his own convenience. But the reader knows, and the fable context demonstrates, that he is only an animal, or object—a small and vulnerable and relatively insignificant part of the general scheme of things.

The small and envious rat, distressed by the superior bulk of an enormous elephant, declares, with the all-too-human bravado of wounded vanity: We little rats are just as good as those great corpulent elephants. He is quickly put in his place by a cat who happens to be perched on top of the elephant (VIII 15). This is a basic mechanism of La Fontaine's fable humor: his mockery of literary, social, and political conventions; his mockery of man himself in his relation to the surrounding universe. It is directly opposed to imaginative poetry, for it aims not at a willing suspension of disbelief but at a suspension, whether willing or not, of our habitual beliefs about ourselves. It is nevertheless a type of humor that can be expressed only through a poetic use of language: it is only by using poetic figures of speech, and the fable is essentially such, that one can express two different and contradictory meanings at the same time. It might be called counterpoetry.

The single vision of imaginative poetry imposes a strong resemblance, sometimes amounting to an exact identity, on two apparently different situations—an idea and an object, an emotion and an experience, a state of mind and what T. S. Eliot has called its "objective correlative." The counterpoetry of La Fontaine's fables gives way to imaginative poetry, or what might be called "poetry proper," when, as in the introductory verses of the heron fable, La Fontaine fuses the two terms of the fable metaphor, when we no longer see the man behind the animal but a single dimension of existence. The fable fiction at this point acquires a certain degree of reality as a poetic intuition. As La Fontaine, perhaps referring back to his earlier reflections about "Aesop's lies," remarks in the introduction to the ninth book of fables:

> Et même qui mentirait
> Comme Esope, et comme Homère,
> Un vrai menteur ne serait.

> And, indeed, if one can lie
> Like Aesop, and like Homer,
> One is not a real liar.

In the fables themselves what we have called La Fontaine's counterpoetry and his poetry proper are less distinct than an abstract analysis suggests. The one implies an intellectual criticism of life; the other, an emotional response to life. But—and this is one of his great qualities as a poet—La Fontaine's intellect and his emotions were closely integrated, not separate or warring faculties. The double vision of comedy is constantly narrowing down to the single vision of imaginative poetry; the single vision of imaginative poetry splitting into the double vision of comedy. In many cases a single passage may be read from either point of view, like a wallpaper that may be seen in either diagonal or horizontal patterns. One might, for example, expect La Fontaine's animals to be comic, or fictitious, in their speech; imaginative, or true, in their physical attitudes or movements. But speech, in La Fontaine's fables, can often be interpreted as a physical attitude or movement; a physical attitude or movement as a form of speech.

La Fontaine's whole vision of reality, his counterpoetry and his poetry proper, became deeper, broader, more assured and closely integrated as he gradually developed his art. The fundamental objective of his fable poetry shows through in the early as well as in the later fables. La Fontaine, in the *Epilogue* to the eleventh book of fables, retrospectively defines it: to translate "the voice of nature," as expressed by all living things, into "the language of the gods," or poetry.

The Fable Language

The counterfiction of the fable would reasonably demand a
sort of counterlanguage for its expression. One would not expect
the fox and the crow to use the formal idiom of Malherbe and
Racine. La Fontaine needed a more informal style, something
approaching the quality of ordinary, everyday speech.

Here is an important source of La Fontaine's fable humor.
His basic narrative style is so constructed as to seem a natural
speaking voice, one that avoids, and consequently exposes, all
recognizably literary effects. Poetic forms and figures of speech
acceptable in a more suitable context appear contrived, preten-
tious, unnatural in the fable. We are made highly aware that
people do not ordinarily go around calling each other "le phénix
des hôtes de ces bois"—the phoenix of the denizens of this forest.

T. S. Eliot once observed that "Every revolution in poetry is
apt to be, and sometimes announces itself to be, a return to
common speech." And, one might add, every revolution in poetic diction exposes the previous idiom, which it supplants, as
a literary, or written, style. Such revolutions are unlikely to occur unless the existing idiom is in a fair way of becoming literary in and of itself, of becoming so restricted and conventionalized as to convey the quality of a written rather than a spoken
language. The effect depends to some extent on how the idiom
is being used. Racine, for example, was able to give the rigid,
highly formalized language of late seventeenth-century poetry the

immediacy and fluency of actual speech. Still, this language, at the very moment it was reaching its apogee in Racine, had elsewhere begun to die. It was to remain moribund until a century later, when it was revitalized by Chénier and Lamartine.

English poets faced with a similar crisis at the end of the eighteenth century favored a revivifying plunge into the language of popular speech. This going to the people, whether in politics or in poetry, is never as easy as it seems. Wordsworth's most strenuous efforts in the direction of popular diction are responsible for some of his worst poems: that mawkish pseudo simplicity—the idiot mother talking about her idiot boy—that Coleridge and Lewis Carroll were quick to spot. A poet, if he is to succeed in supplanting a formal written diction with a popular spoken diction, must do more than imitate the quality of popular speech, which is very likely to be diffuse and inarticulate. He must discover the essential style of popular speech as it has developed through the ages, what might be called the universal language of popular speech. Some poets have found this style in old folk songs or ballads. La Fontaine, since he was using the fable, naturally hit upon a different vein: the age-old language of the folk saying or the proverb.

La Fontaine had perhaps considered and rejected an alternative, for him a tempting one: to imitate the language of sixteenth-century fable writers like Corrozet and Haudent. This archaic style, which Voiture had popularized, was all the rage in contemporary salon poetry and it appealed to La Fontaine, who often used it in his contes. As he writes in one of his fables (IV 11):

Tel, comme dit Merlin, cuide engeigner autrui,
    Qui souvent s'engeigne soi-même.
J'ai regret que ce mot soit trop vieux aujourd'hui:
Il m'a toujours semblé d'une énergie extrême.

He, as Merlin says, who wants to trick another,
  Often tricks himself.
I'm sorry this saying is too old-fashioned today:
It has always seemed particularly vigorous to me.

Sixteenth-century French is less archaic than Merlin's French, which dates back to the thirteenth century. But, since it was no longer a living language, it was subject to the same limitations. It could no longer be used without, as in La Fontaine's contes, creating an effect of literary pastiche. The timeless language of the proverb, though it has a definitely archaic flavor, had survived in La Fontaine's day, and it survives today, as a spoken language.

In abandoning the diction of contemporary poetry for proverb language La Fontaine, as he later pointed out in his *Epître* to the Bishop of Soissons (1687), was following a famous classical precedent, a precedent previously followed by Régnier: Horace's satire style. The Roman satire, like the French fable, was an indigenous, popular, and emphatically nonliterary medium. It was a form that lent itself to the familiar proverb, folk-saying style of speech that Horace adopted, deliberately turning his back on the Hellenistic conventions then current in Latin poetry. Furthermore, Horace and Régnier had each interpolated a fable into one of his satires: Régnier, the fable of the lioness, the wolf and the mule (in La Fontaine, the fable of the horse and the wolf [V 8], and the fable of the fox, the wolf, and the horse [XII 17]); Horace, the fable of the town mouse and the country mouse (in La Fontaine, the fable of the town rat and the country rat [I 9]).

One can imagine that La Fontaine would have given particular attention to these two rare examples of fable poetry. He must, for example, have been struck by Régnier's easygoing, popular style which, breaking away from the formal and somewhat coldly academic vein of Phaedrus, adapts the Greek fable to the indigenous tradition of the French fabliau.

Horace's fable of the country mouse and the town mouse may well have shown La Fontaine some of the further possibilities of fable poetry. Like La Fontaine, Horace conveys a combined human and animal reality in the movements and conversations of his little rodents. Like La Fontaine, he exploits the sound patterns of the familiar proverb style and, again like La Fontaine, parodies more ambitious types of poetry against the background of this style. The town mouse's majestically Epicurean argument in favor of city life is an excellent parody, by anticipation, of some of Horace's later odes: "all terrestrial things are mortal and, whether we be great or humble, there is no escape from death." The nocturnal setting of the trip to town is evoked in traditional epic style: "Iamque tenebat / Nox medium caeli spatium" ("And now night was holding sway over the middle part of the sky").

La Fontaine's version of the fable (I 9), which is known to be one of his earliest efforts, antedating by several years most of the other fables published in 1668, is unusually perfunctory and conventional—an indirect tribute to Horace perhaps. It is hard to do something that has already been done so well. But La Fontaine's fastidious heron (VII 4), as he himself points out, is imitated from Horace's city mouse, who so disdainfully rejects the simple fare provided by the country mouse.

La Fontaine mastered the traditional proverb style so well that his personal inventions, like the songs in Shakespeare's plays, often sound like the anonymous creations of authentic folk literature (I 10): "La raison du plus fort est toujours la meilleure" ("Might makes right"). We know this comes from one of La Fontaine's fables; but we do not quote it as if it were a verse of poetry. We repeat it in exactly the same way that we would say "Handsome is as handsome does" or "The more haste the less speed." With certain expressions—for example (III 1), "contenter tout le monde et son père" ("to please everybody and his father")—even the experts are unable to tell us whether La Fontaine was using an existing phrase or whether he invented a phrase that subsequently was absorbed by the French language.

La Fontaine's fable language is by no means limited to proverbial sayings of the kind; on the contrary, its range is wide and varied. Yet his over-all style, which is clearly recognizable, reflects certain fundamental characteristics of the French proverb or folk-saying style of speech—the same use of grammatical short cuts; the same preference for concrete as opposed to abstract terms; the same exploitation of sound patterns based on alliteration, assonance, internal rhymes, and the repetition of key words or syllables; the same general enjoyment of language for the sake of language.

This is the exact obverse of formal, written French as established by Malherbe and others of his kind in the early seventeenth century. Formal French, with its precise and standardized vocabulary and syntax, its preference for abstract or general terms, its distaste for obvious or striking sound patterns, admits no love of language for the sake of language. It is, ideally, a clear and unobtrusive window through which the meanings of words may be seen with maximum facility and accuracy.

An important objective of the seventeenth-century language reform was a detailed redefinition and sifting out of the existing vocabulary which would eliminate all possible ambiguities and overlappings of meaning. Malherbe believed there was no such thing as a synonym. Popular language will frequently say the same thing over in two or three different ways for the sheer fun of it—a trick that is typical of La Fontaine (IV 11):

Un rat plein d'embonpoint, gras et des mieux nourris . . .

A rat, nicely rounded, plump and well-nourished . . .

La Fontaine also deliberately cultivated the ambiguities of language that his contemporaries took such pains to avoid. He often uses words in such a way as to bring out a double meaning or a hidden pun. In describing a hermit rat who lived in a Dutch cheese, he remarks (VII 3):

> La solitude était profonde,
> S'étendant partout à la *ronde*.

> The solitude was profound,
> Spreading everywhere *around*.

An ox "ruminates" before speaking (X 1). (Christina Rossetti used the same pun in *Eve*.) A loquacious "pie," or magpie, is identified as "notre agasse" (XII 11); the more familiar word points to the verb "agacer," to annoy someone, get on his nerves. The ant's speech, in the fable of the fly and the ant (IV 3), is based on a series of puns on the word "mouche"—fly, beauty spot, parasite, spy.

Another important contribution of the seventeenth-century language reform was its ruling against the elision of what the historian Brunot called "tool words"—articles, pronouns, and prepositions. La Fontaine's deliberate violation of the ruling often gives his style the faintly archaic quality of proverb language (X 13): "Fortune aveugle suit aveugle hardiesse" ("Blind fortune follows blind audacity").

Proverb language here reflects its Latin origins. French proverbs, which were often imitated from corresponding Latin proverbs, tended to retain Latin constructions that had elsewhere fallen into disuse. From the point of view of grammatical precision the reformers, intent on freeing French from Latin influences, were probably right. The French language, since it is less highly inflected, cannot, like Latin, afford to dispense with uninteresting little "tool" words. From the standpoint of poetry their elision has important advantages that La Fontaine was quick to recognize: it creates a more unified and rapid speech unit and throws the full weight of the sentence on the crucial nouns and verbs. Claudel, an active opponent of formal French, observed: "What is called a misuse of the French language is more often the instinctive movement of the language, seeking a short cut through the detours, the obstacles, or the cacophony the pedants have put in its way. Grammatical errors are generally remedies to euphonic errors."

Such short cuts are particularly appropriate in proverb speech but La Fontaine often uses them for other purposes. A protracted series of events may, for example, be summed up in a brief, telegraphic notation, as with the struggle between a spider and a housemaid (III 8):

> Une servante vient balayer tout l'ouvrage.
> Autre toile tissue, autre coup de balai . . .

> A housemaid comes and sweeps the whole fabric away.
> Another web woven, another stroke of the broom . . .

In certain cases La Fontaine's elisions convey a sense of haste; in other cases, a special emphasis. Thus the reformed miser (X 4):

> Il retint tout chez lui, résolu de jouir,
> Plus n'entasser, plus n'enfouir.

> He kept all (his money) at home, resolved to enjoy himself,
> No more piling up, no more burying.

To be grammatically correct this should read "de ne plus entasser, de ne plus enfouir" and the object—money—should be supplied. La Fontaine's omission of the preposition and displacement of the negative not only makes a smoother verse, it gives it the emphatic quality of a solemn oath. And his omission of the object expresses the irrational, compulsive quality of the miser's previous behavior. La Fontaine uses the latter device in his three-word biography of another miser (XII 3): "Un homme accumulait" ("A man was accumulating").

Another typical proverb characteristic of La Fontaine's "Fortune aveugle suit aveugle hardiesse" is its somewhat unusual syntax. The general idea expressed is that unadvised audacity will produce unhoped-for results. But fortune, the logical object, is here the subject; and audacity, the logical subject, is here the object. The inverted syntax has the effect of animating and, particularly in conjunction with the adjective "blind," personifying the abstract noun "fortune." It is true that formal poetry also personifies abstract ideas, but this is a far more explicit procedure, generally involving elaborate metaphors or allusions to the classical deities. As Boileau put it:

Chaque vertu devient une divinité:
Minerve est la prudence, et Vénus la beauté.

Each virtue becomes a divinity:
Minerva is prudence, and Venus beauty.

In the language of the proverb it is not merely the abstract concept but the word itself that comes to life, and the effect is created not by explicit metaphors and classical allusions but by the word's function in the sentence. As with Shakespeare's "And all our *yesterdays* have lighted fools the way to dusty death," abstract concepts acquire concrete identities and seem to be engaging in concrete actions.

The popular tendency toward concrete language, here, goes hand in hand with the popular indifference to logic and grammar. The expression "contenter tout le monde et son père," whether or not we owe it to La Fontaine, derives its special flavor from the incongruous attribution of a particularized paternity to the abstract and supposedly all-inclusive "everybody." Malherbe would certainly have disapproved of the expression; nor would he have approved of using verbs and adjectives as if they were nouns, in certain instances proper nouns. But this is traditional usage in the language of the proverb: "Like the cat in the adage, letting I dare not wait upon I will"; "Handsome is as handsome does"; "Un tiens vaut mieux que deux tu l'auras" ("One yours is better than two you'll have its" or "A bird in the hand is worth two in the bush").

La Fontaine, who quotes this last proverb in one of his fables (V 3), is an excellent noun maker in his own right. A wealthy financier regrets that "le dormir" (sleeping) is not for sale like "le manger" (food) and "le boire" (drink) (VIII 2). The French verbs to eat and to drink are often used colloquially as nouns; "le dormir" was coined by La Fontaine, a particularly apt invention since it reflects the financier's instinctive tendency to view the desirables of life, even so elusive a thing as sleep, as tangible objects that can be bought and sold. Three shipwrecked voyagers (X 15) are identified as "les trois échoués aux bords de l'Amérique" ("the three stranded-on-the-coast-of-America")—a typical Latin participial construction. Here the short monosyllables of verbal argument are metamorphosized into dramatis personae (VI 20):

Elle [Discord] et Que-si-que-non son frère,
Avecque Tien-et-mien son père.

She and It-is-not-it-is-so her brother,
With Thine-and-mine her father.

Another striking characteristic of La Fontaine's "Fortune aveugle suit aveugle hardiesse," and one that contributes greatly to its authentic proverb flavor, is the sound pattern created by

the repetition of the word "aveugle." Proverbs and folk sayings
are often based on sound patterns involving a repetition of key
words or syllables; and it is often sound, as opposed to meaning,
that seems to have dictated the choice of words. This is particularly obvious in redundant expressions that have no real purpose
other than that of establishing an agreeable sound pattern. La
Fontaine is full of little phrases of the kind: "bel et bien," "bon
et beau," "tout seul et sans témoins." (The first two phrases correspond to English expressions like "well and good" and "fine
and dandy." The last means "all alone and without witnesses.")
He also uses the sound patterns as a principle of poetic structure
—a practice theoretically condemned in formal poetry. Malherbe
blue-penciled all the verses in Desportes's sonnets containing
alliteration and internal rhymes.

La Fontaine occasionally uses a somewhat jarring alliteration
for its deliberate shock value (I 10):

Tu seras châtié de ta témérité.

You will be punished for your temerity.

The relentless succession of *t*'s is harsh, but intentionally so, as
Ferdinand Gohin has observed. La Fontaine's wolf is talking to
a lamb that he is planning to devour.

Like the "rhétoriciens" of pre-Ronsardian poetry, like Victor
Hugo, La Fontaine enjoys playing with words (V 5): "*Que* nous
sert cette *queue?*" ("What good is this tail?") asks the fox who
has lost his tail or (II 14):

Un lièvre en *son gîte songeait*
(Car que faire en un gîte, à moins que l'on ne songe?)

A hare was meditating in his hole
(For what can you do in a hole except meditate?)

La Fontaine's parenthetical remark adds to the joke. He seems to be defending himself against possible criticism of his pun but at the same time raises the question: is the poet referring to phonetic or environmental affinities?

Except in special instances of this kind, La Fontaine creates delicate and harmonious sound patterns based on a skillful combination of repeated and contrasting sounds. He is particularly fond of the "mirror" structure of his proverb "Fortune aveugle suit aveugle hardiesse" where the pleasure of oral recognition is increased by the inverted order of recognition. In the proverb this is a question of sentence structure as well as sound. The repeated adjective follows the first noun and precedes the second noun, another characteristically Latin construction. When La Fontaine is imitating the traditional proverb style he often uses such a pattern (IV 22):

> Nos amis ont grand tort, et tort qui se repose
> Sur de tels paresseux . . .

> Our friends are much mistaken, and mistaken those who rely
> On such lazy people . . .

The *t-s s-t* pattern of "tout seul et sans témoins" (III 1) is a pure sound pattern and one that La Fontaine frequently uses in his fable poetry (VII 16):

> Du *pa*lais d'un jeune *la*pin
> Da*me be*lette un *beau ma*tin
> S'empara . . .

> Of a young rabbit's palace
> Dame weasel one fine morning
> Took possession . . .

and (III 1):

La feinte est un pays plein de terres désertes.

Simulation is a country full of uninhabited regions.

The harmony of La Fontaine's most melodious verses, to be sure, rests on a more intangible relation of consonant and vowel sounds (II 12):

Le long d'un clair ruisseau buvait une colombe . . .

Along a limpid streamlet a dove was drinking . . .

and (VI 21):

Sur les ailes du Temps la tristesse s'envole . . .

On the wings of Time sadness takes flight . . .

and (IV 19):

Le dédale des cœurs en ses détours n'enserre
Rien qui ne soit d'abord éclairé par les dieux.

The labyrinth heart in its detours encloses
Nothing not previously known to the gods.

Proverb style is here refined almost to the point of invisibility. One tends rather to think of other kindred lines of poetry:

Et rose elle a vécu ce que vivent les roses . . .

And rose she lived what roses live . . .

and

Et les fruits passeront la promesse des fleurs.

And the fruits will exceed the promise of the flowers.

La Fontaine, though he broke almost all of Malherbe's rules of poetry, always admired and at one time attempted to imitate Malherbe's poetry. Perhaps his delicate inverted sound patterns imply a reminiscence of certain of his former master's most harmonious verses.

The Fable Verse Form

A formal diction is generally accompanied by a regular verse form, an informal diction by a flexible verse form. The formal language of English poetry goes hand in hand with the heroic couplet; the formal language of French poetry, with the classical alexandrin. When Victor Hugo "put a Phrygian bonnet on the dictionary" he simultaneously "broke" the alexandrin.

Flexible meters, like informal dictions, are often justified as a return to the more natural quality of ordinary speech. Corneille, writing in 1650, observed that the occasional stanzas of his *Andromède* were more natural than the alexandrins because their inequalities seemed nearer to ordinary speech—a curious observation since the stanzas in Corneille's other tragedies are invariably reserved for the moments of lyric intensity. Two centuries later Hugo remarked: "A broken verse is admirably suited to receive the proportion of prose that dramatic poetry must admit."

Some have likewise assumed that La Fontaine's irregular verses are a concession to the prosaic character of the fable. Did he himself not assert that the irregular verses used in certain contes are particularly appropriate because they have "a very prose-like air about them"? But what is true of poetic diction is equally true of poetic meters. A poet who succeeded in approximating the prose rhythms of ordinary speech would be making scant use of the actual resources of poetry. In fact he would not be writing poetry at all.

The prose elements in poetry, although they constitute a conscious departure from existing conventions of poetry, still exist within and derive their character from the basic convention of poetry itself—the existence of an underlying schemata that sets up a number of predictable, or anticipated, effects. Dissonance, dissymmetry, irregularity are powerful agents in a poem; they are recognizable only when they are supported by a framework of fairly stable conventions. Poets revolt against an existing convention when it becomes so familiar that it no longer produces the desired effect; their conscious irregularities often give it a new and unexpected power.

T. S. Eliot has remarked that English free verse is a "renewal" of the old form as well as "a preparation for new form." Auden writes that "our problem in the twentieth century is not how to write iambics but how not to write in them from automatic habit when they are not to our genuine purpose." Mallarmé, in his answer to Jules Huret's inquiry on contemporary literature and in his reflections on the contemporary "verse crisis," observed a parallel situation in late nineteenth-century France. Free verse, he explained, is a conscious departure from the classical alexandrin for the purpose of revealing this glorious but outworn form in a new and more arresting light: "The official verse should only be used in moments of spiritual crisis; contemporary poets have understood this very well; with a very delicate sense of reserve, they have wandered around it, approached it with a singular timidity, one might say some terror, and, instead of making it their principle and their starting point, have suddenly made it leap forth as the climax of the poem or of the period!"

The principle works more freely in Mallarmé's later poetry than in La Fontaine's fables, but it is still the same principle. The whole art of La Fontaine's fable poetry, an art that might, on the face of it, seem perilously close to prose, is the art of expressing intangible shades of meaning through a discriminate violation of the existing rules of the game. As such it is actually a direct, though illegitimate, descendant of Malherbe's reforms.

A primary factor in the convention of French poetry is that the French language, which has no tonic accent, does not provide the metrical patterns of stressed and unstressed syllables that English poets adapted from Greek and Latin meters. Technically speaking, French prosody is based not on the number of stresses but on the number of syllables included in a verse. The accent, or beat, is not, as in English poetry, built into the phonetic structure of the words; it is solely determined by the grouping of the words as sense units. The last full syllable (i.e., not final *e*'s) in any group of words forming a single sense unit is accented. These accents are far less emphatic than the accented syllables of English poetry, merely a slight prolongation of the accented vowel sound and, as Alan Boase has pointed out, a rise or fall of melodic pitch.

The twelve-syllable alexandrin, which is about as long a breath as the French language can easily take, is the verse form generally used in serious poetry—the French counterpart of the English iambic pentameter. The English pentameter is a fairly flexible form which, in view of its powerful iambic beat, can afford numerous metrical irregularities and frequently dispense with rhyme; the more subtle foundations of French prosody impose a fairly rigid code of laws on the alexandrin.

A classical alexandrin has four beats. Two of these, which are generally stronger than the others, occur regularly on the sixth and final syllables of the verse. This means that an alexandrin must be so constructed as to have a natural pause at the exact center and again at the end of the verse, and the more emphatic the pause the stronger the alexandrin. Any displacement of these two accents breaks the rhythm of the alexandrin and, according to the rules of formal prosody, is strictly proscribed.

A regular and easily recognizable rhyme scheme is another important factor, the verse form being most apparent with the traditional couplets of alternately masculine and feminine rhymes. As Ronsard, who first popularized the French alexandrin, observed: "The composition of Alexandrins must be grave, proud, and (if one may use the expression) 'altiloquent,' since they are longer than the others and would smack of prose if they were not composed of choice words, grave and resonant, and with a rhyme that is rich enough . . . to remain in the ear until the end of the next verse, which is long."

The classical alexandrin, which Giraudoux has called "that beautiful breathing exercise," corresponds fairly exactly to the regular rise and fall of human respiration. This is why it is so powerful a form, one that no French poet can entirely ignore. At the same time the imperious binary pattern is bound to predominate and impose itself on all things. The alexandrin is the slow beat of a bird's wings, rising and falling waves, a boat riding on the waves—those three recurring images of nineteenth-century poetry. Or it is the yes and no of inner conflict, a pattern that, with Corneille, is still close to rhetoric but, with Racine, translates the actual movement of the passions. It is too powerful, too simple a form to express the more varied and subtly graduated rhythms of human, or natural, existence.

Like any difficult verse form, the classical alexandrin has one great danger: it is far easier to observe a set of technical rules than to grasp the essential spirit of a form. Under these circumstances the celestial music of the alexandrin degenerates into a mere symmetrically balanced rhetoric or, still worse, a stupefying drone. As Claudel once remarked, "It is not always easy to hypnotize people, but it is very easy to put them to sleep."

In France the late seventeenth century was, by common consent, a period particularly lacking in the sense of lyric poetry. In addition, the poetic theory of the time, which tended to think in terms of clear and easily intelligible precepts, placed undue emphasis on technicalities. It had been Malherbe's weakness as a critic that, despite a wonderful ear for the alexandrin, he seemed to believe that the secret of the verse form lay in the degree of rigor governing its prosody. It is his love of discipline, not his ear, that often seems to predominate, as in his demand that a rhyme must rhyme in its spelling as well as in its sound. Boileau, who had little sense of lyric poetry, unhesitatingly followed Malherbe's lead so that his definition of the alexandrin is given entirely in negative terms: no uneven caesuras, no weak rhymes, no run-on lines.

This, as Mallarmé once observed, is the same sort of lowest common denominator that prevails in legal codes: honesty is defined as abstention from theft. And if one is incapable of discovering the law for oneself it is doubtful that one will be able to observe it very successfully. Small wonder that toward the end of the century those who aspired to something more than mere technical correctness should have considered the alexandrin as great a tyranny as the cramped and desiccated language of poetry —a striking example of that "verse crisis" Mallarmé believed endemic in French poetry.

Strangely enough, La Fontaine, who is known primarily for the irregular verses of the fables, was the one lyric poet of his time to have revealed the full melodic potential of the alexandrin. As Valéry suggests, he would probably not have used the irregular verse form so successfully had he not previously mastered the alexandrin. La Fontaine had studied Malherbe, who with his unerring ear for the different tonalities and cadences of the French language, as well as his sheer technical virtuosity, was probably the best example to follow in the arduous haute école of the classical alexandrin. But Malherbe's stately and relatively rigid alexandrin, as adapted by La Fontaine, becomes lighter, sweeter, more fluid and melodious—an evolution that may be due to La Fontaine's familiarity with Virgil's Latin hexameters. Dido's final pleas to Aeneas no doubt inspired the melodic line of Venus's last farewell to Adonis, gliding so smoothly and easily over the underlying metrical structure.

Mon amour n'a donc pu te faire aimer la vie!
Tu me quittes, cruel! Au moins ouvre les yeux,
Montre-toi plus sensible à mes tristes adieux;
Vois de quelles douleurs ton amante est atteinte!
Hélas! J'ai beau crier: il est sourd à ma plainte.
Une éternelle nuit l'oblige à me quitter . . .

So my love was unable to make you love life!
You leave me, cruel boy! At least open your eyes,
Show a little more feeling for my sad good-bys;
See with what grief your mistress is stricken!
Alas! why should I shout? he is deaf to my lament.
An eternal night compels him to leave me . . .

Valéry has pointed out that this passage anticipates "the tone, the sequences, the monumental profile, the very sonority" that we admire in Racine's best tragedies—a parallel that may be explained, as Valéry suggests, by Racine's familiarity with La Fontaine's *Adonis* or, as seems equally probable, a similar encounter with Virgil's Dido.

The passionate, sustained legato of Virgil's Dido, La Fontaine's Venus, Racine's Bérénice—a tone these earlier poets always attributed to female characters—was to become the predominant melody of nineteenth-century poetry at its very best. Modern readers, who are strongly conditioned by nineteenth-century poetry, are thus sometimes tempted to look for this melody in La Fontaine's fables. But the tone of Venus's lament, however beautiful, is not the characteristic tone of La Fontaine's maturity. In his fables La Fontaine will no longer use this neutral, indefinite vocabulary, these evenly balanced cadences, these soft elastic syllable endings that make each word blend imperceptibly into the next. His verses, liberated from the imperious systole and diastole of the human respiratory system, will have a sharper outline, a more distinctly articulated movement. They will no longer be tied together by the force of accumulated momentum; they will be governed by the laws of action and reaction, flux and reflux. In other words, human emotion will no longer be a powerful subjective impulse; it will become an objective fact among many other equally important facts.

In choosing the irregular verse form for his fables La Fontaine was following a current fashion popularized, along with the vogue for archaic forms and mannerisms, by salon poets like Voiture and Sarasin. Free, or irregular, verse, as used by seventeenth-century poets, is not the same thing as the free verse of late nineteenth-century poetry, which dispensed with rhyme and meter altogether. Each verse has a conventional number of syllables, generally the eight- or twelve-syllable verses most familiar to the French ear; each verse is rhymed. But the poet is free to vary the verse lengths and the rhyme scheme as he pleases and may also take certain liberties with established rules of versification, particularly as regards caesuras, weak rhymes and run-on lines. The English language equivalent would be the irregular verses of Milton's "Lycidas" or, among contemporary poets, Frost's "After Apple Picking" and Eliot's "Preludes" and "The Love Song of J. Alfred Prufrock."

So loose a verse form can easily generate a quality of negligent facility as insipid in its way as the pseudo naïveté of neoarchaism —a weakness apparent in the verses that Voiture, Sarasin, and La Fontaine as well, were in the habit of composing on casual social occasions or in letters to their friends. This air of nonchalant extemporaneity, which seemed to put the poet on a footing with the honnête homme, was no doubt the very quality that appealed to La Fontaine's contemporaries. Like the madrigal, another loose form, irregular verse was a wonderful vehicle for the Molière type of literary marquis who took special pride in his amateur standing and boasted of his ability to write verses without ever having learned to do so. La Fontaine himself boasted that the irregular verses of his contes had "a certain air of negligence" that was necessary in the genre.

La Fontaine's fables, though they use certain techniques of informal salon poetry, are free of both the archaic "cuteness" and the negligent facility then characteristic of the genre. We know from surviving manuscripts that La Fontaine polished the irregular verses of his fables as carefully as he polished the alexandrins of *Adonis*. The casual, gentlemanly form is here transformed into a delicate precision tool, a tool particularly suited for La Fontaine's purposes.

One important advantage of an irregular verse form is that, when properly used, it provides an effective built-in gearshift. That poetry does not function consistently in high gear, that there are inevitable moments of lesser intensity, is generally recognized in poems of any length, particularly in dramatic poetry. In the tragedies of Shakespeare and Racine, for example, one may distinguish the recitatives from the arias and, between the quasi-prose of the recitative and the pure song of the aria, a middle voice of melodious, rhythmic speech. These various levels may also be discerned, less obviously perhaps, in shorter poems—a temporary sacrifice of the full effects of poetry in preparation for an ensuing climax. A poet can shift from one level of intensity to another within the conventions of a regular verse form, but irregular verse permits a more powerful, a more rapid, and at the same time a smoother transition.

There is little, if any, recitative in Milton's "Lycidas"; even so, the alternation of three-beat and five-beat verses at the end of the invocation creates a slower, more hesitant movement, previous to the swing into lyric poetry:

> For we were nurst upon the self-same hill,
> Fed the same flock, by fountain, shade, and rill.

There is very little aria in the "Love Song" of Eliot's Prufrock which, for the most part, oscillates between a melodious, reflective middle voice and inspired doggerel; but how beautifully the suppressed song at last breaks free:

We have lingered in the chambers of the sea
By sea-girls wreathed with seaweed red and brown
Till human voices wake us, and we drown.

The built-in gearshift of the irregular verse form is particularly useful in La Fontaine's fables, which, being a form of dramatic poetry, demand many different tones and levels of intensity; and, being short, demand proportionately frequent and rapid shifts from one tone or level to another. La Fontaine's recitative, obtained either by using prosaic, matter-of-fact octosyllables or by breaking the natural rhythm of the alexandrin with displaced caesuras and run-on lines, serves an important function as a vehicle for direct exposition. It is a way of dispatching pedestrian necessities as rapidly and easily as possible. With any form of poetry that demands a certain amount of preliminary explanation, and the fable is such a form, this is no doubt the wisest course. There is nothing more tedious than a writer who feels obliged to use the full resources of poetry to inform us that two characters happened to meet in the street. For La Fontaine, who is easily bored by complicated plot mechanisms, an offhand treatment is particularly advisable. In the fable of the hare and the tortoise (VI 10), for example, he glosses over the practical arrangements of the race as follows:

> On mit près du but les enjeux.
> Savoir quoi, ce n'est pas l'affaire,
> Ni de quel juge l'on convint.

> The stakes were placed near the goal.
> Never mind what they were,
> Or what judge was chosen.

The unpretentious octosyllables are exactly what was needed for the forthright "let's get this over with quickly" attitude expressed. Had La Fontaine been using classical alexandrins he would have sounded perfunctory and, consequently, a bit ridiculous. We can see this with similar short cuts in *Adonis* which have an air of undignified haste:

Il est temps de passer au funeste moment
Où la triste Vénus doit quitter son amant.

It is time to get on to the fatal moment
When unhappy Venus must leave her lover.

La Fontaine's recitative, as Gohin has observed, is also an effective way of picking a piece of direct discourse out of the matrix of indirect narration, as with the neighborly criticisms of the various modes of locomotion used by the miller and his son who are taking their donkey to the fair (III 1):

L'enfant met pied à terre, et puis le vieillard monte,
Quand, trois filles passant, l'une dit: "C'est grand'honte
Qu'il faille voir ainsi clocher ce jeune fils . . ."

The child dismounts, then the old man gets on,
When, three girls happening by, one says: "It's a perfect shame
To have to see that young son limping along like that . . ."

The girl's speech, which must be read as an uninterrupted sense unit, skips over the natural pauses at the end of the second alexandrin and the middle of the third.

La Fontaine thus reserves the full power of the "official verse" for the conclusion of the fable, where the miller, exasperated beyond all endurance, declares that he will no longer pay any attention to what anybody says:

"Je suis âne, il est vrai, j'en conviens, je l'avoue . . ."

"Very well, I'm an ass, I agree, I admit it . . ."

The emphatic rhythm of the concluding verses, almost a clenched fist pounding on the table, gives a very satisfactory ring to the miller's final declaration of independence.

La Fontaine's irregular verses are equally well adapted to the moments of greatest lyric intensity. Arias, or songs, generally use verses shorter than those ordinarily used in poetry, or a palpitating, and highly emotional, alternation of two uneven verse lengths. Corneille, to achieve an aria effect, must abruptly interpolate his stanzas into the alien context of his alexandrin couplets. La Fontaine, like Milton, can construct his irregular verses as arias. This is particularly obvious in his operas. The opening verses of *Galatée*, as set to music by Lambert, became a very popular song. La Fontaine often creates the same aria effect in his fable poetry. Like many other librettists, he sometimes gives his arias a stronger beat by reiterating the same construction in two uneven verse lengths; the romantic (IX 2):

> J'ai quelquefois aimé; je n'aurais pas alors
> > Contre le Louvre et ses trésors,
> Contre le firmament et sa voûte céleste . . .

> Once I was in love; I would not then,
> > Not for the Louvre and its treasures,
> Not for the firmament and its celestial vault . . .

and the intensely agitated (VII 2):

> Les valets enrageaient, l'époux était à bout:
> "Monsieur ne songe à rien, monsieur dépense tout,
> > Monsieur court, monsieur se repose."

> The valets were fuming, the husband depleted:
> "Monsieur considers nothing, monsieur spends everything,
> > Monsieur runs around, monsieur lies down."

The first, which is from the conclusion of the fable of the two pigeons, has something of Cherubino's palpitating love songs to the world in general in Mozart's *Marriage of Figaro*; the second, which is from the fable of the unhappily married husband, recalls Figaro's infuriated last-minute outburst against women. The Mozart analogy is fairly arbitrary, but a useful reminder that arias can convey many different shades of emotion: grief or elation, comedy or drama, and, as with Mozart's Figaro and La Fontaine's husband, an explosion of pent-up exasperation.

The middle voice of poetry, rising to occasional passages of song or dropping into recitative, is, as might be expected, La Fontaine's predominant voice. The irregular verse form is here used not to sink below or soar above the classical alexandrin but to distort or vary the familiar rhythm. Sometimes La Fontaine makes fun of the "official verse" by the unexpected leap from a sonorous alexandrin to a businesslike octosyllable, the built-in timing of a misplaced caesura or a run-on line. At other times he builds more fluid rhythms around it: a gradual crescendo or decrescendo, a slow acceleration or deceleration, a sudden stop or start or change of gear, a climax or an anticlimax.

La Fontaine often uses an octosyllable in combination with an alexandrin: the shorter verse length can either lead up to or away from the alexandrin; it can anticipate or echo, or yet again prolong the movement of the alexandrin; a regular alternation of the two verse lengths creates the palpitating movement La Fontaine so often uses in his arias.

He also obtains a great variety of effects by changing the rhythm of the classical alexandrin. A typical La Fontaine rhythm is an alexandrin divided into three unequal, instead of two equal, parts. This triple division is particularly characteristic of traditional proverb speech: "the lame, the halt, and the blind"; "neither fish nor flesh nor good red herring"; " by land, by sea, and in the air." We often find it in the titles of La Fontaine's fables: "Le chat, la belette, et le petit lapin" ("The cat, the weasel, and the little rabbit"); "Le cochet, le chat, et le souriceau" ("The young cock, the cat, and the little mouse"); "Le lion, le singe, et les deux ânes" ("The lion, the monkey, and the two donkeys"); "Le renard, le singe, et les animaux" ("The fox, the monkey, and the animals"). It is true that the fable subject in each case suggests the triple enumeration; but La Fontaine is careful to preserve the characteristic proverb rhythm by saving the longest word for the final term or, if it is no longer than any of the others, adding an adjective or a diminutive.

In his fable poetry La Fontaine sometimes uses the structure for its cumulative effect. The enormous elephant who excites the envy of a small rat is surmounted by an important sultaness (VIII 15):

> Son chien, son chat et sa guenon,
> Son perroquet, sa vieille, et toute sa maison . . .

> Her dog, her cat and her monkey,
> Her parrot, her duenna, and her entire establishment . . .

The build-up is partly due to the expansion, in the alexandrin, of the rhythm established in the preceding octosyllable. But it is supported by the rhythm itself. An evenly accented verse suggests a rocking motion: the two halves refer back and forth to each other in an eternal equilibrium. An asymmetrical, triple division creates a sense of forward motion: each term progresses to the next. La Fontaine also uses it when he wants to convey a sense of rapid movement, in this case the evolution of the Duc de Bourgogne's kingly genius (XII 1):

> Il ne va pas, il court, il semble avoir des ailes.

> It doesn't go, it runs, it seems to have wings.

La Fontaine's asymmetrical structure, although less frequent in other poets, is technically within the limits of classical prosody since the all-important caesura remains in its rightful place. Racine occasionally uses it to convey a sense of internal agitation. For example Hermione's

> Où suis-je? Qu'ai-je fait? Que dois-je faire encore?

> Where am I? What have I done? What have I yet to do?

At the same time Racine's 3-3-6 division is smoother than La Fontaine's habitual 2-4-6 and 4-2-6 divisions.

La Fontaine's displacement of the two fixed accents at the caesura and the final syllable of the verse, which is definitely out of bounds, has a recognizable shock effect. For example (VII 10):

> Perrette là-dessus saute aussi, transportée.

> Whereupon Perrette also skips, transported.

So does the caesura (from the sixth to the ninth syllable) and, consequently, the alexandrin. His run-on lines, which displace the final accent of the verse, serve a large variety of purposes. In some cases the run-on line conveys an impression of haste, as with the frenetic family-raising activities of the lark who postponed the "pleasures of love" until the season was nearly over (IV 22):

> Elle bâtit un nid, pond, couve et fait éclore
> A la hâte . . .

> She built a nest, lays, broods and hatches
> In a hurry . . .

In other cases it conveys a sense of surprise, as with the sudden snap of an innocent-looking oyster (VIII 9):

. . . car l'huître tout d'un coup
Se referme . . .

. . . for the oyster suddenly
Closes . . .

A regular succession of displaced accents creates a counterpoint
of rhyme and meter. La Fontaine's description of a perilous sea
voyage, as Gohin has observed, is a good example of the process
(VII 12):

Celui-ci, pendant son voyage,
Tourna les yeux vers son village
Plus d'une fois, essuyant les dangers
Des pirates, des vents, du calme, et des rochers,
Ministres de la mort.

This man during his voyage,
Turned his eyes toward his village
More than once, enduring the dangers
Of the pirates, the winds, the lull, and the rocks,
Ministers of death.

Technically speaking, the sentence consists of two octosyllables,
one decasyllable, and one and a half alexandrins—a structure conveyed orally by the rhyme scheme. From the standpoint of sense
units, hence metrical accents, the structure is totally different. A
number of divisions are possible but the most natural would
probably be one octosyllable followed by three alexandrins:

Celui-ci pendant son voyage,
Tourna les yeux vers son village plus d'une fois,
Essuyant les dangers des pirates, des vents,
Du calme, et des rochers, ministres de la mort.

The resulting counterpoint of rhyme and accent is particularly appropriate for a navigator contending with tumultuous and hostile forces; but it is pleasing in itself, just as the counterpoint of melody and meter is pleasing in a Chopin waltz.

La Fontaine's word patterns provide another variable which can either support or oppose the natural movement of the alexandrin (III 1):

La feinte est un pays plein de terres désertes.

Simulation is a country full of uninhabited regions.

The sound pattern here coincides with the meter. La Fontaine's description of a heron produces a syncopated effect (VII 4):

Un jour sur ses longs pieds allait je ne sais où
Le héron au long bec emmanché d'un long cou.

One day on his long feet ambled I don't know where
The heron with the long beak jointed into a long neck.

La Fontaine has reduced the always incredible anatomy of the heron to three quick lines: first the long legs, then the long beak, then the long neck into which the beak is jointed. ("Emmanché" suggests a metal blade fitted into a wooden handle.) The characteristic double-jointed gait of the heron, co-ordinating the assorted fragments, is created by the emphatic repetition of the crucial monosyllable *"long"* on the offbeat accents immediately preceding the caesuras and the rhyme and by the offbeat internal rhymes, "allait," "sais," "emmanché" echoing the downbeat "pieds." The heron is actually dancing a slow-motion, six-beat rumba.

No amount of generalization can cover the full range of La Fontaine's versification and specific instances are inevitably distorted when abstracted from their specific contexts. One can only hope to indicate the general character and scope of his technique and to show the importance of this technique not only as an aesthetic form but as a means of indirect communication.

There are two tones of voice that La Fontaine especially disliked, whether in life or in poetry: the thick HA HA HA of the heavyhanded joker—or "rieur," as La Fontaine calls him (VIII 8); and the blind, headlong rush of uncontrolled emotion. His personal tone of voice has a quality which, for lack of a better word, is generally called "naïveté." In effect it is the exact reverse of naïveté as the word is generally used: the art of suggesting meanings without actually spelling them out. The movement, as well as the language, of La Fontaine's poetry is an important key to these buried meanings: the dead-pan humor, the contained emotion, the hidden sting, the secret joy—the whole tightly woven fabric of poetry and counterpoetry.

III

The Fable as Counterpoetry

The Poetic Comedy

Certain poets start out by imitating, others by satirizing, their predecessors. La Fontaine followed the two courses simultaneously. He spent about half his time writing conventional poetry and the other half, in his fables and certain other poems as well, making fun of the conventional poetry that he had written. This is what makes his poetic satire so penetrating. La Fontaine is not making fun of his elders in the same way that the youthful Rimbaud made fun of François Coppée. He is making fun of La Fontaine, and other poets like La Fontaine, trying to imitate their elders.

During the years 1659 through 1661 La Fontaine, on the strength of his heroic idyl *Adonis*, hired himself out to the great financier Fouquet. It was during this period that he wrote his uncompleted *Songe de Vaux* as well as a number of incidental poems in honor of Monsieur and Madame Fouquet and various members of the royal family. In a letter to Fouquet La Fontaine refers to them, in apparent self-deprecation, as his "poetic pension": in return for Fouquet's protection he will duly acquit himself of an appropriate piece of poetry each quarter. The poems themselves—pompous odes in the manner of Malherbe (for the royal family), archaic ballads in the manner of Voiture (for the Fouquet family)—are conscientious efforts to fulfill his part of the agreement. Here is the very situation that La Fontaine described in his comedy *Clymène*, which, though undated, was written either during the Fouquet period or, as Philip Wadsworth believes, a little later.

The scene is set on Parnassus, where a bored and impatient Apollo complains that he no longer hears any good love poetry and abruptly commands his Muses to see if they can do a little better. The reluctant Muses successively produce an amoebian eclogue, a pathetic and then a comic dialogue, an archaic ballad, a Malherbian ode, a Horatian lyric, and a gallant poem in the style of Voiture.

The various efforts of the Muses are correct, ingenious, and fairly elegant, the only obvious failure being that of Calliope, the Muse of epic poetry, who breaks down completely after the first stanza of her ode. As with the sonnet in Molière's *Le Misanthrope*, which was applauded as genuine poetry when the comedy was first performed, the satire is discreet. It is no less devastating for this: a merciless inventory of all the principal clichés of late seventeenth-century love poetry. The theme is always similar: the complaint of an ardent lover whose "severe" or "cruel" mistress offers him friendship rather than passion. The tone is always similar: a hyperbolic submission of all natural and divine phenomena to the adored object.

Taken in and of themselves the parodies might not seem particularly amusing. The comedy is created by the dramatic context which contrasts the mechanical made-to-order quality of the poems, as revealed by Apollo's abrupt commands and the embarrassed objections of the virgin Muses, with the pretended ardor of the poems themselves. Erato's imitation of Voiture, for example, is punctuated by the following dialogue with Apollo:

> ERATO (who is anxious to get the whole thing over with as soon as possible):
>> Mais n'est-ce point assez célébré notre belle?
>> Quand j'aurai dit les jeux, les ris, et la sequelle,
>> Les grâces, les amours, voilà fait à peu près.

APOLLO (who insists on a thorough job):
> Vous pourrez dire encor les charmes, les attraits,
> Les appas.

ERATO: Et puis quoi?

APOLLO: Cent et cent mille choses.
> Je ne vous ai compté ni les lis, ni les roses;
> On n'a qu'à retourner seulement ces mots-là.

ERATO: But haven't I glorified our beauty enough?
> When I've mentioned the tricks, the smiles, and the
>   rest,
> The graces, the cupids, that will be about it.

APOLLO: You could also mention the charms, the seductions,
> The lures.

ERATO: And then what?

APOLLO: A hundred million things.
> I have listed neither the lilies nor the roses.
> One has only to juggle those words around.

If a cliché be defined as a poetic figure unsubstantiated by the appropriate emotion, this is an excellent illustration of the phenomenon. And the best part of the joke is that La Fontaine is here describing the very procedures used in his *Songe de Vaux*, his "poetic pension" and, later, in his *Psyché* and his pastoral operas, which veritably pullulate with "jeux," "ris," "grâces," "amours," and the invariably cosmetic roses and lilies.

"Contre ceux qui ont le goût difficile" ("Against those who are hard to please"), which introduces the second book of fables, carries the same device a little further. The theme is taken from Phaedrus's seventy-second fable, where Aesop, in response to a critic's contempt for the playful fable, steps forward in the cothurn, or thick-soled boot, of tragic drama and imitates the opening verses of Euripides's *Medea*. Phaedrus's satire is directed primarily against the mendacious hyperboles of tragic poetry, the implication being: the playful fable is no more fictitious than the most ambitious types of poetry. La Fontaine uses the idea in his introductory verses:

> Le mensonge et les vers de tout temps sont amis.

> Lies and verses have always been friends.

The poem itself, like *Clymène*, is aimed less against the fundamental conventions of serious poetry than against their misuse. The satire is a little broader than in *Clymène* and La Fontaine's irregular verses allow him to adapt his form more closely to the meaning of his satire, to use rhyme and meter, as well as figures of speech, as a source of comedy. This is the precarious, drunken precision of the clown on the high wire—an art that demands still greater balance and control than that of the acrobat himself.

La Fontaine, speaking in his own person, takes over the servile function of the Muses and pretends that he is trying to please a number of critics who despise the puerility of "Aesop's lies."

> Censeurs, en voulez-vous qui soient plus authentiques
> Et d'un style plus haut? En voici. Les Troyens,
> Après dix ans de guerre . . .

> Critics, do you want something grander
> And in a more elevated style? Here goes. The Trojans,
> After ten years of war . . .

The contrast between the mechanical production and grandiloquent pretensions of the poem, conveyed in *Clymène* by the alternation of Apollo's instructions and the Muses' performance, is here built into the structure of the verse. La Fontaine's recognition of the critic's demand for a more elevated type of poetry, contained in the first verse and the first half of the second verse, results in one and a half respectable classical alexandrins which prepare the reader for more of same. From here on all

is chaos. La Fontaine's announced compliance—"En voici"—
which has the extreme brevity of colloquial speech and the key
word of his attempted epic—"Les Troyens"—are crowded, with
startling economy, into the second half of the second verse. This,
like the lark's last-minute family, is definitely a crash job—a particularly incongruous effect in view of the ambitious nature of
the assignment: a description of the stratagem of the wooden
horse which is roughly imitated from Virgil's summary of the
events leading up to the fall of Troy (*Aeneid* II 13-20).

Exposition is always the least interesting part of epic poetry.
Virgil's account is no more than a necessary prelude to the great
drama of Troy's destruction and he wisely treats it as such, using a concise, matter-of-fact, narrative style. La Fontaine treats
the exposition as if it were a highly dramatic event. Virgil's ten-
word summary of the Greek dilemma becomes:

> Les Troyens,
> Après dix ans de guerre autour de leurs murailles,
> Avaient lassé les Grecs, qui, par mille moyens,
> Par mille assauts, par cent batailles,
> N'avaient pu mettre à bout cette fière cité . . .

> The Trojans,
> After ten years of war about their ramparts,
> Had tired the Greeks, who, with thousands of means,
> Thousands of attacks, hundreds of battles,
> Had been unable to break down that proud city . . .

Virgil's straightforward "by the divine art of Athena" becomes:

> . . . par Minerve inventé
> D'un rare et nouvel artifice . . .

> . . . invented by Minerva
> An unusual and novel stratagem . . .

And Virgil's over-all reference to the Greek leaders chosen to hide in the horse expands into a full-fledged epic enumeration:

> le sage Ulysse,
> Le vaillant Diomède, Ajax l'impétueux . . .

> prudent Ulysses,
> Valiant Diomedes, hotheaded Ajax . . .

The rapid summary of events is thus strained to the bursting point with inappropriate poetic ornaments.

It is true that Latin lends itself to concise narration more easily than French; but La Fontaine's translation could hardly be more awkward. Virgil's account, which is broken down into several sentences, is eight verses long. La Fontaine's parallel account consists of an extremely long and complicated sentence, thirteen verses long, uninterrupted by any real grammatical break. If it consisted entirely of alexandrins it would be more tolerable, but La Fontaine uses a mixed form where two alexandrins are regularly followed by an octosyllable. The alternation of the two verse lengths produces an uneven, pulsating rhythm. Each time the octosyllable recurs the tempo seems to be slowing down; the relentless alexandrins, which follow on its heels, each time restore the original tempo. The general effect is that of a man continually attempting to stop for breath and continually being prevented from doing so.

A critic's eventual objection thus conveys a literal truth:

> "C'est assez, me dira quelqu'un de nos auteurs;
> La période est longue, il faut reprendre haleine."

> "That will do," one of our authors will tell me;
> "The period is long, you must take a new breath."

La Fontaine had a special distaste for protracted and complex narratives. In his mock-heroic treatment of a battle between the vultures and the pigeons he remarks (VII 8):

> Si je voulais conter de point en point
> Tout le détail, je manquerais d'haleine.

> If I tried to make a point-to-point account
> Of all the details, I would be out of breath.

In French literary parlance the expression "lack of breath" also connotes a lack of the poetic imagination and vitality necessary to sustain an extended or ambitious theme. La Fontaine's satire is actually aimed not at Virgil but at himself and, perhaps, at certain of his contemporaries as well. You see, he seems to be telling us, what would happen if I tried to write in Virgil's epic style.

The same effect of absurdly rapid compliance with his critic's demands recurs in the second portion of the poem. In response to the not unreasonable objection—you are unsuited to write in such an elevated style—La Fontaine obligingly switches to a pastoral theme:

> Eh bien! baissons d'un ton. La jalouse Amarylle
> Songeait à son Alcippe . . .

> All right! let's lower it one notch. The jealous Amaryllis
> Was thinking of her Alcippus . . .

La Fontaine's prefatory remark that he is descending *one* notch (no more, no less, for gallant or burlesque poetry would have been lower still) is perhaps a dig at the rigid seventeenth-century hierarchy of poetic genres that Boileau described, a few years later, in his *Art poétique*.

La Fontaine (and he always did have a weakness for pastoral poetry) is beginning to have rather a good time with his shepherd and shepherdess and sheep and zephyrs when he is rudely interrupted. The hard-to-please critic, who is reminiscent of Malherbe blue-penciling Desportes's airy sonnets, contests the legitimacy of a rhyme. At this point La Fontaine gives up in despair. It is impossible, no matter how hard you may try, to please other people, he concludes—with the implication: therefore I might as well stop trying.

The role La Fontaine here assumes—a willing but unenthusiastic poet submitting to the demands of established literary authority—is a role he sometimes played in real life. Take, for example, his description of the boar hunt in *Adonis*. The hunt begins with a long list of the names and attributes of the participants, all the major heroes of Greek mythology. The passage is imitated from Ovid's description of the warriors assembled to hunt the Caledonian boar (*Metamorphoses* VIII), which, like Virgil's review of the Latin warriors banded together against the Trojans (*Aeneid* VII), is imitated from Homer's enumeration of the Greek warriors marching against Troy (*Iliad* II). As might easily be expected, each imitation is a little inferior to its predecessor. The ritual enumeration, perfectly in keeping with the epic simplicity of Homer, tends to embarrass a more sophisticated poet. Virgil is less at his ease than Homer; Ovid sounds a bit like a mythological social register; La Fontaine is completely undone.

At times he is too emphatic; at times he is too perfunctory; at times he seems inclined to give up in despair:

Cent autres que je tais, troupe épaisse et confuse . . .

A hundred others who shall be nameless, a thick and jumbled troop . . .

Then he takes a new breath—any enumeration of this kind must include one beautiful Amazon—and continues:

Mais peut-on oublier la charmante Aréthuse . . . ?

But can we forget the charming Arethusa . . . ?

Another difficulty, which La Fontaine shares with Ovid, is the incongruity of assembling an army of Homeric warriors for what appears to be a fashionable hunting party. The only thing that can justify the build-up is a monster of truly epic ferocity. It is here that La Fontaine fails most completely and most delightfully by unintentionally betraying a certain amount of sympathy for the supposedly abhorrent occupations of his monster:

Au fond du bois croupit une eau dormante et sale:
Là, le monstre se plaît aux vapeurs qu'elle exhale;
Il s'y vautre sans cesse, et chérit un séjour
Jusqu'alors ignoré des mortels et du jour.

Deep in the woods lies some stagnant, dirty water:
There, the monster enjoys the vapors it exhales;
He wallows in it ceaselessly, and cherishes an abode
Hitherto unknown to mortals and to daylight.

It is the suppressed note of sensual satisfaction that undoes La Fontaine's monster. Water, darkness, silence, solitude—these are always magical themes for La Fontaine. The appropriate reaction of horrified disgust is displaced by potent memories of forbidden childhood pleasures: how delicious to wallow about like this in the ooze! From now on our hearts are no longer in the right place. Had La Fontaine written the passage in the past tense and delayed it until the end of the poem it might well have turned into a rather touching piece of elegiac poetry.

La Fontaine's sudden shift of perspective, so fatal to his description of the boar hunt, is written into the very structure of the fable, and this for a very good reason. It is of the essence of the epic that one particular action, the action the poet has undertaken to relate, should seem of special and overwhelming significance. It is of the essence of the fable that no single action should seem of any more significance than any other. Each separate event, whatever its relative size or weight, is viewed in the light of a larger, weightier, transcendent whole—a point well illustrated in one of La Fontaine's last fables (XII 21). The elephant, who is planning to make war on the rhinoceros, assumes that Jupiter's monkey has come down from Olympus to witness the impending battle. "What battle?" the monkey asks. "I came down here to divide a blade of grass among a few quarrelsome ants."

Imagine that Jupiter had commanded the monkey to write an epic poem about the battle between the elephant and the rhinoceros. The result would be rather similar to the description of the boar hunt in *Adonis*. La Fontaine, like Jupiter's monkey, has a certain twist of mind that prevents him from looking very long or very steadily at what are generally considered serious events. And when obliged, even by his own poetic strategy, to treat the weighty themes that deep within himself appear so trivial he will, whether consciously or unconsciously, adopt an attitude of perverse resistance conducive to high comedy.

This situation, explicitly stated in "Contre ceux qui ont le goût difficile," is more subtly conveyed in the fable proper. Unlike certain other practitioners of the mock-heroic vein, La Fontaine never underlines his own jokes. The satire is expressed in delicate incongruities which the reader must discover for himself. For example, an exterminating cat—a second Rodilardus, the Alexander of cats, the Attila or scourge of the rats, a veritable Cerberus—was feared, La Fontaine tells us, and in a perfectly neutral tone of voice, for *one* league around (III 18)! A rather

abrupt return to rodent scale. And his epic treatment of the bat-
tles of minor rodents or of various barnyard massacres is in itself a pungent commentary on the heroic magnification of human violence.

As with "Contre ceux qui ont le goût difficile," La Fontaine's
mock-heroic fables generally refer to the traditional epic theme,
apparently Virgil's version, of the Trojan War: the valiant but
unavailing efforts of a chosen band of rat heroes, Artarpax, Psi-
carpax, Méridarpax (Breadthief, Crumbthief, and Little-pieces-
thief) against the overwhelming might of the conquering weasels
(IV 6); the carnage perpetrated by a Greek-seeming fox who
manages to make his way into a henhouse at dead of night when
everybody is asleep (XI 3). Sometimes the parallel is only suggested; at other times it is explicitly brought out (XI 3):

> Tel, et d'un spectacle pareil,
> Apollon irrité contre le fier Atride
> Joncha son camp de morts . . .

> Thus, and presenting a similar spectacle,
> Apollo outraged against the proud Atrides
> Littered his field with dead . . .

The first verse would seem a deliberately heavy version of a
characteristic Virgil comparison; the verb "joncher," generally
used for branches, flowers, or little fragments, a deliberately
heightened translation of the Latin "sternere" (to spread out,
strew) a verb that Virgil sometimes uses in such a context.
La Fontaine, whether intentionally or unintentionally, is actually parodying his own not-too-successful imitation of Virgil
(*Aeneid* II 364) in *Adonis*:

> C'est ainsi qu'un guerrier pressé de toutes parts
> Ne songe qu'à périr au milieu des hasards:
> De soldats entassés son bras jonche la terre . . .

It is thus that a warrior attacked on all sides
Thinks only of dying in the midst of perils:
With piled-up soldiers his arm litters the ground . . .

The already somewhat extravagant "joncher" becomes still more grotesque when used as a noun, as in the matter-of-fact (IV 6):

La principale jonchée
Fut donc des principaux rats.

The principal litter
Thus consisted of the principal rats.

La Fontaine's use of the word "gent" to identify different tribes or nations of fable animals would, likewise, seem a humorous allusion to the Latin "gens" or "genus," words that Virgil often uses in the *Aeneid*. In at least one instance, La Fontaine's parody is aimed less at Virgil than at a contemporary imitation of Virgil. "La gent qui porte crête," or crest-bearing people, of the fable of the two cocks (VII 13) presumably refers to "La gent qui porte le turban," or turban-bearing people, of Malherbe's ode to Anne of Austria upon her return to France.

The implications of La Fontaine's "gent" or "peuple" are also complicated by Virgil's use of the Latin "genus," which refers to different nations of people in the *Aeneid*, to refer to different species of animals in the *Georgics*, and without ironic overtones. The Latin word can apply equally well to either. "La gent qui porte crête" implies a parody of Malherbe's official style. But "le peuple aquatique" (X 3), or ocean people, is a direct translation of Virgil's "genus aequoreum" (*Georgics* III 243).

The mock-heroic vein is a traditional vein of satire, and it was a popular one during the years that La Fontaine wrote his early fables. Parodies of epic poetry, modeled on Scarron's *Virgile travesty*, were all the rage during the 1660's. But, epic poetry being then a particularly weak and timid genre, they lacked the stimulus of a good contemporary target. It is a good deal of a liability to be reduced to satirizing poetry as distant as Virgil's *Aeneid* must have seemed to La Fontaine's contemporaries. One feels the same lack in La Fontaine's mock-heroic poetry which, for all his deft and witty treatment of the familiar themes, adds little to his numerous predecessors in the genre. It is not surprising that his most original and penetrating parodies are aimed rather against the pastoral genre—the most flourishing of seventeenth-century forms and one that attracted La Fontaine himself considerably.

The fable, though it is not often used for this purpose, is actually no less inimical to the pastoral elimination of physical violence than to the heroic enlargement of physical violence. The traditional pastoral décor of streamlets, flowers, zephyrs, and sheep takes on a very different cast when viewed, however appreciatively, by a hungry lion (IV 12).

La Fontaine's treatment of the oyster in the fable of the oyster and the rat carries the same point a little further (VIII 9):

> Une s'était ouverte, et bâillant au soleil,
> Par un doux zéphyr réjouie,
> Humait l'air, respirait, était épanouie,
> Blanche, grasse, et d'un goût, à la voir, nonpareil.

> One of them had opened, and gaping at the sun,
> Gladdened by a gentle zephyr,
> Sniffed the air, breathed, stretched in joyous abandon,
> White, plump, and to judge from her looks, most delectable.

This—with its succulent liquid consonants, its soft vowels, its pulsating rhythm leading up to the final mouth-watering alexandrin—is a highly erotic piece of poetry. The décor and general manner are again borrowed from pastoral poetry. We seem to see the white and palpitating body of a sleeping nymph, her clothes disarranged by the breezes, stretched out in an attitude of voluptuous abandon. The description, though far more intense, is reminiscent of a sleeping nymph in *Le Songe de Vaux*: "The Zephyrs had turned back a bit of the linen that covered her breasts. . . . I shall not undertake to describe either the whiteness or the other marvels of these beautiful breasts, nor the admirable proportions of the bosom, easily discernible despite the linen, which a soft breathing occasionally caused to swell."

The whole trick to this sort of thing, as practiced by La Fontaine and his contemporaries, is to charge the innocent pastoral theme with as much erotic suggestion as it can hold and then disappoint the reader by a last-minute reversion to propriety. We can see the formula at work in the concluding section of *Clymène*, where La Fontaine, using his nom de Parnasse, "Acante," describes what purports to be a tremendous amorous victory: Cupid allows him to kiss any portion of the sleeping Clymène that he chooses. After a protracted guessing game with the virgin Muses, which lends itself to a variety of jokes and also keeps the expectant reader on the hook, La Fontaine reveals that he chose (how could anyone *dream* I might have been guilty of indelicacy!)—her foot. The La Fontaine of *Le Songe de Vaux*, in similar vein, engages in a long internal debate: is it fair that my eyes should have the monopoly of this inviting spectacle? As was to be expected, "fear" and "respect" eventually prevail and the overexpectant reader is again put in his place.

La Fontaine's ambiguous treatment of his oyster-nymph, at once a succulent food and an attractive sexual object, leaves no room for such refinements. What do I see, cries the straight-to-the-point rat: this is some victual! Unlike the well-behaved swain of pastoral poetry, he immediately pounces on his prey, and with disastrous results. The oyster-nymph, unlike the nymphs of pastoral poetry, has a traplike shell that closes with a bang.

Another pastoral convention flatly contradicted by the fable is the assumption that human lamentations, when loudly and extensively proliferated in desolate environments, are to be viewed with sympathy and commiseration. The assumption is valid only to the extent that the reader identifies himself with the lovesick shepherd or shepherdess. If, whether by accident or design, he is invited to assume the role of a detached observer his reaction is very different. La Fontaine had already fallen afoul of this general law in his description of Adonis's despair at Venus's departure for a neighboring temple:

Et, soit que des douleurs la nuit enchanteresse
Plonge les malheureux au suc de ses pavots,
Soit que l'astre du jour ramène leurs travaux,
Adonis sans relâche aux plaintes s'abandonne;
De sanglots redoublés sa demeure résonne.

And, whether from their pains enchantress night
Plunges the unhappy with the juice of her poppies,
Whether the morning star brings back their labors,
Adonis ceaselessly gives way to his complaints;
His habitation resounds with redoubled sobs.

La Fontaine is off to a good start with the lyric and somewhat Virgilian evocation of succeeding nights and days; but his abrupt descent from the general to the particular, in the final couplet, is at the same time too perfunctory and too emphatic. The spell is broken and the atmosphere of gentle melancholy displaced by the highly inappropriate thought: what a terrible amount of noise!

This unintentional, though—given La Fontaine's personal love of peace and quiet—understandable, effect is deliberate in La Fontaine's description of a mother lion mourning her young (X 12):

La nuit ni son obscurité,
Son silence et ses autres charmes,
De la reine des bois n'arrêtait les vacarmes.
Nul animal n'était du sommeil visité.

Neither night nor its obscurity,
Its silence and its other charms,
Could stop the racket of the queen of the forest.
No animal was approached by sleep.

A mother eagle mourning her eggs gets similar treatment (II 8):

Ce second deuil fut tel que l'écho de ces bois
   N'en dormit de plus de six mois.

This second mourning was such that the woodland echo
   Got no sleep for more than six months.

The unsympathetic attitude toward noisy lamentations is here justified by the unimaginative egocentrism of the mourner, in each case a beast or bird of prey. It is nonetheless clear that La Fontaine is constitutionally opposed to any natural or human event calculated to disturb the exquisite delights of sleep, a taste already apparent in his description of the Palace of Sleep in *Le Songe de Vaux*. His enthusiastic description of dawn on the morning of the boar hunt in *Adonis* might well be qualified as the most hypocritical couplet—and this is saying a good deal—in his entire works:

Un matin que l'Aurore au teint frais et riant
A peine avait ouvert les portes d'Orient . . .

One morning when Aurora, of the fresh and smiling cheeks,
Had barely opened the doors of the Orient . . .

La Fontaine's real attitude toward dawn is better conveyed, in *Psyché*, by Cupid's objection: "But she gets up so much too early in the morning!"

This is the point of view in the fable of the old lady and her two servants (V 6), where the rising sun appears, not as the beautiful and welcome sight of literary tradition but as the dreaded back-to-work signal for two young girls who are never able to get enough sleep:

> Dès que Téthys chassait Phébus aux crins dorés,
> Tourets entraient en jeu, fuseaux étaient tirés,
> > Deçà, delà, vous en aurez;
> > Point de cesse, point de relâche.
> Dès que l'aurore, dis-je, en son char remontait,
> Un misérable coq à point nommé chantait.

> As soon as Thetis drove golden-haired Phoebus away,
> Reels began to turn, spindles were twisted,
> > Right and left, it was piling up;
> > No stopping, no respite.
> As soon, I am saying, as dawn remounted his chariot,
> A miserable cock immediately sang.

The about-face from a literary conception of dawn to a working girl's conception of dawn is accompanied by a parallel shift from the flowing alexandrins to the rapid, mechanical movements of reels and spindles. The second figure of speech—"Dès que l'aurore, dis-je, en son char remontait"—seems to indicate a return to literature. But the interjection "dis-je"—a sigh? a yawn? —betrays a vast undercurrent of fatigue and boredom which completely undermines the energetic figure of the sun god leaping into his chariot.

In addition to satirizing prevailing conventions of poetry La Fontaine will sometimes incorporate a specific line of poetry, one that was probably familiar to his contemporaries, into the alien context of his fables. The opening verse of the fable of the lion and the gnat (II 9) is an instance of this type of literary deflation:

> "Va-t-en, chétif insecte, excrément de la terre."
>   C'est en ces mots que le lion
>   Parlait un jour au moucheron.

> "Off with you, puny insect, excrement of the earth."
>   It is in these words that the lion
>   Spoke one day to the gnat.

The initial apostrophe is taken from Malherbe's prudently posthumous attack on Concini:

> Va-t-en à la malheure, excrément de la terre.

> Away to perdition, excrement of the earth.

That La Fontaine's lion is addressing the alexandrin to a gnat is in itself a commentary on Malherbe's poem, his resounding orchestration of the guttural *r*, which Ronsard considered the most heroic letter in the alphabet.

La Fontaine's lion, in striking contrast to the lions of Malherbe's official poetry, is soon reduced to a state of foaming desperation by the methodical and vengeful gnat. The anticlimax is already anticipated by the abrupt descent from the stately rhythms and resounding syllables of the alexandrin to the brisk, narrative tone of the ensuing verses. These businesslike, expositional octosyl-lables, with their ritual "one day," are written in pure fable-ese. In both tone and rhythm they are scarcely distinguishable from prose. It is as if a small but effective muffler has been suddenly ap-plied to the sonorous growl of offended majesty. Lion or no lion, king or no king, alexandrin or no alexandrin, we are hereby warned, this is the fable universe and nothing is sacred any longer.

In his *Epître* to the Bishop of Soissons (1687) La Fontaine also gave an unexpected twist to Malherbe's description of the golden age by applying it to the ornate and mannered salon poetry he had at one time admired:

Tous métaux y sont or, toutes fleurs y sont roses.

All metals there are gold, all flowers are roses.

The transposition of existing lines of poetry was an accepted practice among La Fontaine's contemporaries, but generally only in the case of verses translated from an ancient or foreign language, and it was done without a trace of irony. Boileau's faithful friend, admirer, and editor, Brossette, believed that Boileau always improved on the original, either by correcting the figure or by giving it a more striking and ornate expression. La Fontaine's adaptation of familiar verses to the alien context of his fables is more comparable to the techniques of certain modern poets, in particular Laforgue and Eliot. As is often the case with modern poets, the transposition involves an element of parody; but parody is an effective way of using what would otherwise be an unusable literary instrument. In a sense it is a renewal as well as a rejection of the outworn figures of poetry, and the line between renewal and rejection is not always very clear.

It is significant that La Fontaine generally parodies verses which, although he is unable to take them at face value, he respects as poetry. Legend has it that he experienced his first poetic emotion when, at the age of twenty-two, he heard an army officer declaim Malherbe's ode on the assassination of Henry IV. According to a contemporary, La Fontaine listened to the sonorous rhetoric in a transport of "joy, admiration and astonishment" and forthwith began to read and imitate Malherbe's poetry. The La Fontaine of the fables has outgrown his youthful enthusiasm, but he still respects the talent of his former master.

A more striking example of La Fontaine's semiadmiring, semi-ironic attitude toward his predecessors is the figure borrowed from Virgil in the last couplet of the fable of the oak and the reed (I 22), reputedly his favorite fable:

> Le vent redouble ses efforts,
>   Et fait si bien qu'il déracine
> Celui de qui la tête au ciel était voisine,
> Et dont les pieds touchaient à l'empire des morts.

> The wind redoubles its efforts,
>   And succeeds in uprooting
> Him whose head was once close to the sky,
> And whose feet touched the empire of the dead.

In the second *Georgic* (288-297) Virgil warns that trees must be given plenty of room for their roots, "particularly the green oak which stretches as far towards Tartarus with its roots as towards heaven with its head. Therefore neither winter winds nor stormy rains can overthrow it. It stands unmoved and outlives many generations, seeing many ages of men roll by while it endures." The same figure recurs in the *Aeneid* (IV 441-449) as an image of Aeneas' resistance to Dido's pleas. The oak, as far as Virgil is concerned, is a symbol of heroic impregnability—a symbol that La Fontaine's oak erroneously interprets as a literal fact and that La Fontaine himself demolishes in the final couplet of his fable simply by substituting the imperfect tense for the eternity of Virgil's present. We know that La Fontaine particularly admired Virgil's image. He had previously used it in a letter to his wife, during his Limousin voyage, to describe the twin towers of Amboise. La Fontaine's former patron, Fouquet, had been briefly imprisoned at Amboise and, in the same letter to his wife, La Fontaine described his emotion at visiting Fouquet's tiny cell. Perhaps at that time the image of the oak was deflected to the idea of fallen majesty. The fable of the oak and the reed would seem to apply to the sudden downfall of the powerful financier and patron of the arts. La Fontaine's use of an oak tree, as opposed to the Aesopian olive tree, in this fable also is significant.

What is interesting here is not simply La Fontaine's destruction of the traditional literary figure of the oak but the way in which he did it. Had La Fontaine concluded with an anticlimactic octo-syllable, his habitual practice in deflationary instances of the kind, he would have conveyed a note of vulgar satisfaction. His dignified and intensely lyric alexandrins, as much a tribute to the beauty of Virgil's image as a subtle hint that he, La Fontaine, is unable to take this image at face value, strike exactly the right shade of meaning: I cannot believe, as men may once have be-lieved, that oaks and heroes are invulnerable; but I should greatly prefer to believe they were.

The Social Comedy

Taine, in line with his personal philosophy of literature, interpreted La Fontaine's fables as an accurate picture of seventeenth-century society, from the lion king on down to the plebeian frogs and donkeys. To the extent that any social satire must use the concrete materials of its particular age Taine is certainly justified, and his study frequently illuminating. Social satire would be a far less potent instrument did it not refer, beyond these specific situations, to a more general truth.

Organized society, as seen by the satirist, has always been built on a few fairly simple and unvarying laws, as contrasted with the multitudinous intricacies of individual behavior. La Fontaine, referring to Descartes's theory of the animal machine, remarks: it is the courtiers, not the animals, who are machines (VIII 14). The relative power and skill of the various members will determine the hierarchical structure of the group while the simultaneous play of ambition, envy, greed, and fear will produce a continual jockeying for position within the established hierarchy. It is an unwritten principle of social behavior that these laws should never be openly recognized for what they are. This is why the subject is so well adapted to the double vision of comedy. The essence of successful social comedy lies in the ability to convey the specific patterns of speech by which the unchanging laws of social organization are disguised, yet simultaneously revealed.

The satirist deliberately selects the materials best suited for his particular purpose. And even within this limited range the mechanism is made to appear still simpler, still more mechanical, than it really is: the semiautomatic phrases and gestures, the synchronized responses, the recurring situations that we find in Balzac, in Proust, in Jane Austen, in Trollope, in Dickens. Yet the machinery must not become so crude as to appear implausible; it must be sensed, rather than seen, beneath the recognizable rituals and conventions of prevailing social forms.

The fable, or fiction of the speaking animal, would seem a particularly appropriate medium for social comedy. The animal reality behind the fable offers a striking image of the quasi-animal laws behind the social process. Yet, as in any society, the animal reality is veiled by human words. La Fontaine, with the Chaucer of the "Nun's Priest's Tale," is one of the few poets to have successfully used the fable as an instrument of social satire. This is because, with Chaucer, he is one of the few poets to have brought the fable metaphor to life, to have transcribed the essential animal trait in a recognizably human tone of voice or gesture.

La Fontaine's three principal fable characters, the lion, the fox, and the wolf, are the traditional triumvirate of *Le Roman de Renart*. La Fontaine, who probably knew the medieval epic in one form or another, brought his fable heroes up to date. The lion no longer has the uncertain status of King Noble. He has become all-powerful and has more the character of a natural force that must be manipulated than of a human authority who may be opposed. The fox is no longer a feudal baron, defying the king from his fortified castle, Malpertuis. He has taken up residence at court. The wolf is no longer the king's seneschal. He has turned into the late-Renaissance figure of the pedant.

La Fontaine has also gone a good deal further than the authors of *Le Roman de Renart* in bringing out the original fable metaphor of the animal-man.

The lion, for example, has always been acknowledged as the king of beasts and, to reverse the simile, kings have frequently been compared to lions. The metaphor is so familiar that one seldom stops to look at it closely. The lion would never have been chosen for the role were he not an important beast of prey, but many other animals are beasts of prey. Two additional factors must be taken into consideration. In the first place, the lion seldom exerts himself. As Konrad Lorenz explains: "To put it crudely, the lion is about the laziest of the predatory beasts: he is indeed quite enviably indolent. . . . If the pent-up drive for locomotion urges him, for once, to walk up and down the length of his cage, his movements bear the character of a leisurely after-dinner stroll and have nothing of the frantic haste with which captive canine carnivores discharge their frustrated urge to cover long distances."

In the second place, his gaze is generally fixed on the distant horizon. To go back to Lorenz: "His majesty of bearing . . . is due to the simple fact that, being a hunter of large animals of the open plains, he habitually surveys the far distance and disregards everything moving in the foreground."

The seventeenth-century introduction of the peruke as an essential feature of the royal profile no doubt gave further accuracy to the traditional figure of speech; as compared to the more fundamentally regal bearing of the lion, this is a small detail. Perhaps Louis XIV, in adopting the peruke, was unconsciously trying to look a little bit more like the animal to which his forebears had been so frequently compared.

The kings of France had collected menageries of exotic animals since the time of Francis I, and French poets had had occasion to look at lions. La Fontaine is perhaps the only poet to have divined the specific attributes of royalty behind the traditional image of the lion. Malherbe once apostrophized Louis XIII as follows:

Prends ta foudre, Louis, et va, comme un lion . . .

Take your lightning bolt, Louis, and go, like a lion . . .

There is something a bit incongruous about the whole verse. One simply does not tell the king of France to pick up his lightning and get going. Proper kings—a truth more fully comprehended by Louis XIV than by his father but nonetheless fairly universal— do not pick things up and they seldom, if ever, exert themselves. But neither do lions, and this reveals an error of imagery as well as tone. The demand for frantic haste, induced by Malherbe's indignation at the insurrection of the Protestants at La Rochelle, is inconsistent with the image of the royal lion.

On the other hand, how right La Fontaine is to use Malherbe's verbal annihilation of Concini for his lion's dismissal of a gnat:

"Va-t-en, chétif insecte, excrément de la terre."

The royal hauteur is conveyed not only by the contemptuous character but also by the vagueness of the epithet. The king of beasts, with his habitual disregard for "everything moving in the foreground," will not even deign to recognize what type of insect he is addressing. Granted that a lion can speak, this is exactly the form of speech he would use.

The fox and the wolf, though no less predatory, are smaller. They are also active, sharp-eyed creatures—two characteristics that bar them from any claim to royal blood. These are eager courtiers on the alert for any possible crumb of patronage. La Fontaine's fox, in contrast to the quasi-static figure of the lion, is, both physically and morally, in a state of continual motion. We see him advancing, retreating, insinuating, flattering, ducking a blow here, driving home an advantage there, always adapting his manner to the character and social status of his victims and always proceeding by indirection. The very model of the late-Renaissance courtier, he has thoroughly mastered the art of dissemblance. His courteous and polished discourse betrays no trace of his underlying greed and egoism.

The fox, as La Fontaine himself has pointed out (XI 6), is

not by nature any more cunning than the wolf. It is his close-set eyes, his pointed nose, his neat and rapid footwork that stamp him as a master of social intrigue. The wolf, because of his heavier frame and solemn, doglike face, must assume the necessary role of court pedant and universal fall guy. A figure no less unscrupulous than the fox but somehow lacking the fox's Machiavellian flair for intrigue, he is worsted in every encounter with his more accomplished rival.

The cumbersome, gruff, and ill-co-ordinated bear is of course a lout and a boor, a figure then typified in France as well as England by the rough provincial nobleman unversed in salon or courtly etiquette. His mind works slowly and rarely attains the level of articulate speech. A dangerous companion, an impossible guest, he expresses his simple, forthright emotions in occasional catastrophic gestures.

One could continue the list at considerable length: the arrogant and queenly eagle who has so much in common with the Lady Catherine de Bourgh of *Pride and Prejudice*; the sleek, long-waisted, and rather untrustworthy lady weasel, who also posed for Alisoun in Chaucer's *The Miller's Tale*: "As any wesele hir body gent and smal . . ."; the garrulous and vulgar magpie; the subtle cat; the ubiquitous fly; the unhappy donkey. In each case the human voice exactly transcribes the animal gait or attitude, half-disguising, half-betraying the fundamental animal reality which, after all, is no more than a profound and necessary impulse to maintain, and if possible improve, one's particular position in the universal peck order.

Were La Fontaine merely seeking to convey the fundamental identity of human and animal behavior he would leave little room for comedy. The trick, with La Fontaine, is to suggest simultaneously the important common denominator and the equally important discrepancy: namely, the specifically human need to defend, and also to attack, the existing social order in terms of moral principles. Some view this hopefully as a sign of man's inner aspiration to be a little better than he is; some view it contemptuously as no more than cowardly, self-interested hypocrisy. Others, like La Fontaine, view it with a certain degree of wry amusement. All must agree that this basic need, nearly as important to man as food and drink and shelter, modifies the human situation, whether for better or for worse.

La Fontaine's poetic satire supposes a contrast between the idealized literary theory and the common-sense fable actuality of human existence: here is an animal world, tightly circumscribed by its animal limitations, portrayed as a world of privileged demigods! The illusion, to be sure, was generally directed at a limited segment of French society that could be fairly easily persuaded to accept it at face value: the king, to begin with, and after him the courtiers who basked in his reflected glory. Malherbe once remarked that there are three orders of being that can never be flattered too much: kings, gods, and mistresses. The observation, quoted by La Fontaine in two separate fables, throws a certain amount of light on late seventeenth-century court poetry, religious poetry, and love poetry, which are not always as different as might be expected. The Apollo of La Fontaine's *Clymène* treats the art of flattery as a recognized poetic genre, introduced by Malherbe and Voiture and best illustrated by their two contrasting styles.

When poetry degenerates into the art of flattery the distinction between the poet and the courtier and, consequently, La Fontaine's poetic and his social satire, becomes tenuous. The successful poet must acquire the courtier's flexibility and tact; the successful courtier must acquire the poet's verbal fluency. La Fontaine's most accomplished courtier, the fox, is also the most literary of the fable animals, his speech being generally couched in the insinuating rhythms and ornate figures of poetry. The fox, however, knows very well what he is doing. Whereas La Fontaine's poetic comedy arises out of the absurd pretensions of the servile poet, his social comedy arises out of the credulity of the smooth-tongued courtier's victims.

The art of flattering important people, however gross, demands a certain amount of tact, particularly when the flatterer has a lower social status than his victim. The poetic illusion must be given at least a semblance of plausibility. There are certain delicate situations in which a policy of respectful evasion is best, a point well illustrated in the fable about the lion's court (VII 7).

His majesty the lion has invited delegates from all his subjects to his "Louvre"—an exceptionally malodorous cave. (The proper noun seems highly impertinent. The real Louvre, which suffered from the absence of any proper sanitation, was notoriously evil-smelling. The physical stench pervading the physical splendor of the royal court is, in addition, a fitting image of the crudity and brutality underlying the outward refinements of courtly behavior.) The gruff, outspoken bear, who is among the first to arrive, holds his nose and consequently incurs his monarch's displeasure, a misadventure that results in his immediate execution:

> Sa grimace déplut. Le monarque irrité
> L'envoya chez Pluton faire le dégoûté.

> His grimace was found displeasing. The outraged monarch
> Dispatched him to Pluto to act so squeamish.

The monkey, rushing to the other extreme, proclaims that there is no scent, no flower, that is not as garlic when compared to the odor of the cave. His "idiotic flattery," which comes uncomfortably close to irony, is no more pleasing to the monarch than the discourteous gesture of the bear and invites a similar result. The fox alone, who claims that a bad cold has impeded his sense of smell, survives the difficult test of etiquette.

Back in the rough, soldierly court of Henry IV the bear might possibly have been excused; in the comparatively unsophisticated court of Louis XIII the monkey might even have had a certain measure of success; only as polished and experienced a courtier as the fox could hope to survive for any length of time at the court of Louis XIV where absurdity was almost as fatal a breach of etiquette as outright rudeness. La Fontaine, though not a particularly successful courtier, was well versed in this cold-in-the-head type of evasion, generally expressed as the manifest impossibility of praising a noble patron in adequate terms. The dedication of *Adonis* to Fouquet, for example, reads: "Indeed, your merit reduces us to the necessity of making a very difficult choice; it is difficult to remain silent on the subject, and it is impossible to speak of it in sufficiently worthy terms."

There are other occasions when poetry or, to put it more crudely, flattering reassurances are not only appropriate but directly or indirectly demanded. The fable about the obsequies of the lioness (VIII 14) is an example of direct-demand flattery somewhat similar in character to the demand poetry of *Clymène* and "Contre ceux qui ont le goût difficile." The lion's wife has died and the other lesser carnivores are vying with each other in their passionate expressions of grief—all but a stag whose wife and children were previously devoured by the deceased queen. The lion, on being informed of this, is about to take immediate vengeance. But the stag announces that the death of the queen is no occasion for grief: she herself, appearing to him in a vision, announced that she is now a goddess, living happily with others of her kind in the Elysian fields. The stag, instead of being executed, is handsomely rewarded.

Taine has compared the opening verses of the fable, where the different animals emulate the widowed monarch's ear-splitting expressions of grief, with Saint-Simon's description of a royal funeral; the stag's description of the dead queen's apotheosis with Bossuet's funeral oration for Marie Thérèse, the wife of Louis XIV. Taine's parallel between the hyperbolic behavior of Saint-Simon's courtiers and the howling mimicry of La Fontaine's animals is very apt. But this behavior is equally reminiscent of Malherbe's official poetry. Malherbe, in his ode on the death of Henry IV, claims that he is outmatched by no one but the queen in both the duration and the intensity of his grief—an honorable defeat since her tears are likened to the Seine overflowing its banks.

The real origin of La Fontaine's fable, which is taken from the sixteenth-century Italian fable writer Abstemius, would seem to be the death and deification of the ideal shepherd, Daphnis, a traditional pastoral theme that Theocritus used in his first idyl and Virgil in his fifth eclogue. Perhaps Abstemius was also thinking of Caligula's alleged behavior after his sister's death: he ordered all nonmourners to be executed for their lack of respect and all mourners to be executed for their failure to realize that his sister was a goddess. La Fontaine mentions the anecdote in the fable of the lion's court (VII 7).

It is curious to see how a somewhat implausible convention of pastoral poetry—the sudden about-face from universal lamentation at Daphnis's death to universal jubilation at his apotheosis—was thus transcribed into an actual form of court etiquette. But the fictions of courtly etiquette, in particular the assumption that any royal death is of immediate and overpowering importance to humanity at large, correspond fairly closely to the fictions of pastoral poetry.

As regards the mourner himself, such egocentrism is fairly natural. A person who feels deeply is often hurt by the obvious indifference of his human, even his natural, environment—a wound that has been bared by certain of the Romantic poets. Still, most of us eventually learn that our personal emotions are a good deal less important to others than to ourselves—unless, like the royal personages of La Fontaine's fables, we have been protected from this truth. It is with a sense of astonished incredulity, as well as anger, that the lion king learns that the stag has failed to participate in the universal lamentations. The same naïve egocentrism recurs in the behavior of the mother lion and the mother eagle who, when deprived of their young, keep the whole forest awake for several months.

Untitled animals can ill afford to indulge their personal emotions so freely, a moral exemplified by the sad fate of the mother owl (V 18). (There being no feminine for "hibou," La Fontaine refers to his owl as a "he." I am inclined to believe that "she" was actually a mother.) The owl and the eagle having agreed to live in peace and no longer devour each other's children, the owl fondly describes her baby owls so that the eagle will be able to recognize, and spare, them:

> "Mes petits sont mignons,
> Beaux, bien faits, et jolis sur tour leurs compagnons."

> "My children are darling,
> Beautiful, well-formed, and prettier than any of their friends."

One fine evening the eagle, in search of food, happens on

> De petits monstres fort hideux,
> Rechignés, un air triste, une voix de Mégère.

> Some particularly hideous little monsters,
> Sour-looking, dismal, shrill scolding voices.

These are certainly not the owl's children, she concludes, with greater logic than understanding. The poor owl returns home to find nothing left of her nestlings but their feet.

The owl complains to the gods—a fairly moderate reaction as compared to the hysterical screaming of mother lions and mother eagles—but is deprived of even this small comfort when a kind neighbor remarks: "Can't you see that it's all your own fault?" Owls, like lions and eagles, may have their personal tragedies; they are expected to submit more quietly to the decrees of fate.

Malherbe, who so admired the hyperbolic weeping of Henry IV's widowed queen, shows some irritation at du Périer's prolonged grief over his daughter's death: "Ta douleur, du Périer, sera donc éternelle?" "Is your grief, du Périer, to be eternal?"

The theme of Stoic resignation, as it appears in seventeenth-century poetry, is generally aimed at the Duponts or du Périers of this world. When the courtier-poet is addressing royalty he takes a different tone. His function is not to enlighten but to please, deliberately to encourage and propitiate the naïve egoism so natural to humanity in general, though it survives in its purest form only in certain privileged classes.

The cat, as accomplished a manipulator as the fox, expresses these nuances very well when she sets out to arouse the mutual suspicions of a mother eagle and a mother sow (III 6). The three animals live in the same tree, the eagle at the top, the sow at the bottom, the cat in the middle. The cat first climbs to the top of the tree and warns the eagle that the sow is attempting to uproot the tree. She then runs down to the bottom and warns the sow that the eagle may plunge down at any minute and devour her baby pigs.

La Fontaine took the fable from Phaedrus, whom he follows fairly closely, including the cat's parallel speeches to the eagle and the sow. But Phaedrus's cat addresses the eagle and the sow in very similar terms; La Fontaine's whole comedy lies in the cat's changing inflections of speech. Here is how she addresses the eagle:

> Elle grimpa chez l'aigle, et lui dit: "Notre mort
> (Au moins de nos enfants, car c'est tout un aux mères)
>   Ne tardera possible guères.
> Voyez-vous à nos pieds fouir incessamment
> Cette maudite laie, et creuser une mine?
> C'est pour déraciner le chêne assurément,
> Et de nos nourrissons attirer la ruine."

She climbed to the eagle, and told her: "Our death
(At least that of our children, for it's all one to mothers)
    Is perhaps imminent.
Do you see at our feet, incessantly burrowing,
That cursed sow, excavating a pit?
It is certainly to uproot the oak,
And achieve the destruction of our nurslings."

The necessary appearance of a solidarity of interests is thus established on the very highest level, a moral equivalent to the physical ascension of the tree: "We mothers put our children before everything else."

An outside observer might reply: "Of course you do. This is a natural instinct, as apparent in sows as in eagles." But the whole tone of the cat's speech implies that maternal solicitude is a rare and delicate and extremely disinterested emotion, most keenly felt, no doubt, by mother eagles but also understood by mother cats. It is thus that a person of inferior rank might attempt to influence the behavior of an Andromache. The cat concludes:

"S'il m'en restait un seul, j'adoucirais ma plainte."

"If only one were left me, I should soften my lament."

This highly irrational conjunction of present fact and future possibilities perhaps alludes to the lament of Racine's Andromaque in the tragedy performed a year before La Fontaine published his first volume of fables:

C'est le seul qui me reste, et qu'on veut nous l'ôter.

He is all I have left, and of which they would deprive us.

The physical and social descent to the sow produces the following speech:

"Ma bonne amie et ma voisine,
Lui dit-elle tout bas, je vous donne un avis.
L'aigle, si vous sortez, fondra sur vos petits.
　　Obligez-moi de n'en rien dire:
　　Son courroux tomberait sur moi."

"My good friend and neighbor,"
She whispered to her, "I'll give you some advice.
If you go out, the eagle will swoop down on your children.
　　Be so kind as to keep this to yourself:
　　She would revenge herself on me."

Community of interest is here established by the conspiratorial tone: not "we mothers in league against that repulsive female" but "we underdogs in league against that unscrupulous woman." The show of fellow feeling, assuming the sow is the social inferior of the cat, is in itself a form of flattery and far more effective, here, than a parade of fine maternal sentiments.

We should not conclude that La Fontaine's sympathies lie with the underdog, and read into his fables the egalitarian moralism so typical of eighteenth-century thinking. La Fontaine was far too scrupulous an egalitarian to fall into such an error. A king, undoubtedly, is different from an ordinary person; this does not mean the one is any better or wiser than the other. Human egoism, when unprotected by royal or aristocratic privilege, loses its original childlike candor and is forced into other channels: greed, envy, fear, to name a few. La Fontaine never tells us that one form of egoism is preferable to the other. Royal egoism is certainly the more dangerous of the two but bourgeois egoism is perhaps the uglier. The lion, however cruel and preposterous, is saved from the minor vices by his sublime self-assurance. Like Henry James's Madame de Bellegarde, he exemplifies the dignity which "may reside in the habit of unquestioned authority and the absoluteness of a social theory favorable to yourself." Whatever else may be said of him, he knows how to die (III 14), one of the few notable virtues of the aristocracy of La Fontaine's time.

Suffice it to say that royal egoism is different from bourgeois egoism and must be handled in a different way. To manipulate a king one must propitiate that sense of divine right with which he is so generously endowed; all his personal actions, desires, and emotions must be given an aura of disinterested nobility. To manipulate a bourgeois one may, like the mother cat, appeal to his natural distrust of the powers that be; one may also offer a tempting morsel to his starved and battered but inextinguishable urge for recognition. In the latter case poetry, though poetry of a more crude and obvious variety, is again in order, as with the fox's famous apostrophe to the crow.

A later fable shows us a different facet of the fox's poetic talent. The fox has descended in a bucket to the bottom of a well under the misapprehension that the reflection of the moon is a delicious cheese. The rash, impulsive gesture seems out of character for Aesop's fox. La Fontaine's fox, a poet no less than a schemer, is here deceived by his own imagination (XI 6):

> . . . l'orbiculaire image
> Lui parut un ample fromage.

> . . . the orbicular image
> Appeared to him as an ample cheese.

(Try to find a way of saying "round reflection" that really makes the mouth water. It would be hard to beat La Fontaine's formulation.)

Aware of his mistake, the fox persuades the wolf to repeat the performance in the other bucket so that his own will rise to the surface again:

> "Camarade,
> Je vous veux régaler; voyez-vous cet objet?

C'est un fromage exquis. Le dieu Faune l'a fait,
　　La vache Io donna le lait.
　　Jupiter, s'il était malade,
Reprendrait l'appétit en tâtant d'un tel mets."

　　　　　　　　　　　　　　　"Comrade,
I want to give you a real treat; do you see this object?
It's an exquisite cheese. The god Faun made it,
　　The cow Io gave the milk.
　　Jupiter, if he were sick,
Would recover his appetite tasting such a dish."

The moon-cheese is less substantial than the cheese in the fable of the fox and the crow. The soft *ge, che* and *j* sounds no longer appear at the rhyme. They are hidden inside the verses and are in each case followed by a poignant *i*: "un fromage exquis," "La vache Io," "Jupiter." The successive *t*'s in the last two verses play powerfully upon the nerves. And the mythological references create a certain aura of unattainability. (Keats, always at the height of his powers when describing food, applied a similar figure to a bowl of celestial cream in his *Endymion*.) No wonder the wolf leaps recklessly into the empty bucket.

The fable concludes not with a piece of advice from the fox to the wolf but with a piece of advice from La Fontaine to the reader:

Ne nous en moquons point: nous nous laissons séduire
　　Sur aussi peu de fondement;
　　Et chacun croit fort aisément
　　Ce qu'il craint, et ce qu'il désire.

Let's not laugh at him; we let ourselves be seduced
　　On no less flimsy grounds;
　　It's very easy to believe
　　The things we fear, the things that we desire.

The moral is particularly apposite: the fox's description of the imaginary cheese, however cynical, has the appeal of genuine poetry, an appeal that works almost as strongly on the enlightened reader as it does on the credulous wolf.

The social machinery, so ably manipulated by La Fontaine's fox, is explained, or sanctioned, by another fiction, perhaps another form of poetry, that goes by the name of justice. The difference is that none of the fable characters believe, or even pretend to believe, this kind of poetry. The arguments whereby natural might is conventionalized as natural right are flimsy, half-hearted, and singularly unpersuasive, amounting to no more than an empty ritual which, for some mysterious reason, is considered a necessary preamble to the ultimate triumph of force. The quick-witted fox is the fable poet par excellence; the awkward, slow-thinking wolf assumes the less demanding role of legal counselor.

La Fontaine has devoted a number of different fables to the subject, all pointing to the same conclusion:

La raison du plus fort est toujours la meilleure . . .

The argument of the stronger is always the best (or might makes right) . . .

This famous maxim introduces the fable of the wolf and the lamb (I 10), the story of the wolf's unsuccessful efforts to disguise his natural appetites as a legitimate act of vengeance. He first accuses the lamb of disturbing his drinking water, but the lamb points out that it is drinking downstream from the wolf. "Well, I know that you insulted me last year." But the lamb, who is not yet weaned, was not born at the time. "Then it was your brother." But the lamb has no brothers or sisters. At this point the infuriated wolf abandons all pretense of rationality. "At any rate it was someone connected with you, for you are all against me, you, your shepherds, your dogs. I've heard about it. I *must* have vengeance." Whereupon the wolf carries the lamb off into the forest and eats it without further ado.

The wolf, although he does eventually eat the lamb, does not come off very well in this encounter. The final summation betrays a note of almost neurotic self-pity. One senses that his rage has been worked up to the boiling point by the manifest failure of his successive arguments. His mistake is to have given the lamb any opportunity for rejoinder, to have allowed himself to be diverted from his role of judge to that of party to the dispute. But then the wolf, the most human of the fable animals, is often impeded by his murky conscience: he would like to be able to prove that he is right.

The lion's behavior, though equally unscrupulous, is far more dignified, as is apparent during a brief experiment in communal living with four smaller and nonpredatory animals (I 6). A stag is caught and the lion, counting on his claws, determines that the prey must be divided into four pieces. Thus far the only bar to good faith seems a lack of aptitude for arithmetic. He then proceeds to establish his claim to the first quarter because of his noble blood; to the second quarter, because he is the strongest; to the third quarter, because he is the bravest. As for the fourth quarter:

> "Si quelqu'une de vous touche à la quatrième,
> > Je l'étranglerai tout d'abord."

> "If any one of you touches the fourth,
> > I shall strangle him at once."

The final argument, phonetically no more nor less than an angry roar, is entirely conclusive and contrasts favorably with the anxious fumbling of the wolf.

La Fontaine refers the incident back to "the old days" and the general character of the lion seems to point not to Louis

XIV himself but to one of his ruder forebears. The fable of the animals stricken by the plague (VII 1) shows us how royal justice is dispensed in the more sophisticated atmosphere of the Sun King's court.

The animal world is stricken by a deadly plague and the lion king holds a council meeting to inform his subjects that the divine anger must be appeased by the death of the most guilty of them. In order to induce an atmosphere of free confession he begins with an enumeration of his own misdeeds:

"Pour moi, satisfaisant mes appétits gloutons,
    J'ai dévoré force moutons.
    Que m'avaient-ils fait? Nulle offense.
Même il m'est arrivé quelquefois de manger
      Le berger."

"As for me, satisfying my gluttonous appetites,
    I have devoured a good many sheep.
    What wrong had they done me? No offense.
Sometimes I have even happened to eat
      The shepherd."

The fox quickly protests that the lion is showing too much delicacy of feeling. A sin to eat stupid, vulgar sheep? No, no. What an honor for them to be chewed up by their king! As for the shepherd—well, we all know he is our natural enemy. This general interpretation is eagerly seconded by all present and extended to the various misdeeds of the other beasts of prey. At last the poor donkey comes forward. Emboldened by the general atmosphere of autocriticism and no doubt flattered to be treated on a footing of apparent equality, he eagerly admits that, tempted beyond his means, he once took a mouthful of grass to which he was not properly entitled. His statement is greeted with scandalized cries of horror. A more or less learned wolf quickly demonstrates that the depraved donkey is the cause of all their troubles and he is summarily executed.

La Fontaine's fable refers specifically to court morality, but the same mechanism could be applied to other situations. Dickens used it in *Martin Chuzzlewit:* Mr. Pecksniff, a nineteenth-century British composite of the lion, the fox, and the wolf, informs the rapacious Pecksniff family that their rich relation's innocent young companion is planning to do them out of their expected heritage. The moral outrage of the Pecksniff family, provoked by a crime of which they themselves, not their victim, are actually guilty, is expressed with the same violence and unanimity as that of La Fontaine's carnivores: "In their strong feelings on this point, they, who were agreed on nothing else, all concurred as one mind. Good Heaven, that she should harbour designs upon his property! The strong-minded lady was for poison, her three daughters were for Bridewell and bread-and-water, the cousin with the tooth-ache advocated Botany Bay, the two Miss Pecksniffs suggested flogging."

La Fontaine's conclusion—moral judgments at court (and in other places too) depend entirely on one's relative power or lack of power—expresses the general theme of the fable; the changing inflections of dialogue reveal the actual operation of the law. The donkey *remembers* that he *once,* under *exceptionally* tempting circumstances, took *one* mouthful of grass to which he was not properly entitled. He is no doubt trying to imitate the lion, a characteristic weakness of Aesopian donkeys, but the conscience-stricken tone of his confession, in striking antithesis to the proper royal manner, designates him as a predestined victim.

The lion, unlike the wolf in the earlier fable, freely admits that the sheep he has devoured had done him no wrong. But observe the casual offhand tone; the vaguely globular "*force* moutons" which seems to indicate that exact statistics are unnecessary in so trivial a matter; the equally vague "Même il m'est arrivé *quelquefois* de manger Le berger."

This last sentence, one of the most famous enjambments in French poetry, has given rise to considerable controversy. According to one school of thought, the run-on line expresses the lion's attempt to gloss over his terrible misdeed. Others have objected that the echo rhyme, far from de-emphasizing, gives special emphasis to the crucial "Le berger." Neither interpretation really seems to hit the nail on the head. This use of an alexandrin followed by a run-on echo rhyme has an effect of unexpected finality, like a sudden tennis volley interposing on the regular back-swing forward-swing of a succession of ground strokes. The same device recurs in the fable of the miser whose hidden treasure has been surreptitiously removed (IX 16):

L'homme au trésor arrive et trouve son argent
    Absent.

The man with the treasure arrives and finds his money
    Gone.

This is a particularly neat instance as the unexpected echo rhyme exactly contradicts the meaning of the preceding alexandrin. Dame Fortune, the real heroine of the anecdote, removes the treasure before the miser has time to realize what has happened and enjoys the joke immensely.

But La Fontaine's lion has a terrible innocence about him: it is inconceivable that he should be capable of making a joke, particularly a joke aimed partially against himself. His characteristic tone, here as elsewhere, is one of pure statement of fact. The surprise effect is wholly unconscious and expresses the courtiers' reaction to the lion's open avowal of his occasional consumption of shepherds. His Majesty, without so much as blinking an eyelash, has made a real howler.

One might suspect that La Fontaine and his fable source are anthropomorphizing here. After all, there is some justice in the

fox's argument that the shepherds are the animals' natural ene-
mies. The fable comes nearer to the truth than might be supposed. Observers like Ernest Seton tell us that most wild animals living in the open avoid killing men, unless molested, because they have learned this generally has disastrous consequences.

The lion has indeed committed an appalling blunder and the
fox, as chief public relations officer, must immediately set to
work to drown the unfortunate remark in a sea of hyperbole.
This is clearly a situation in which, as Malherbe remarked, it
is almost impossible for the flattering reassurances of the fox to
seem exaggerated. An object of what might be called "indirect-
demand flattery" he is simply playing back a tape recording of
the lion's implied opinion of himself.

The lion has assumed the role of, in all probability actually
conceives himself as, a just and highly magnanimous monarch
who, in the moment of common peril, voluntarily renounces his
royal privileges and places himself on the same footing as his
subjects. At the same time he is sincerely convinced that he, as
king, can do no wrong—a conviction that heightens the mag-
nanimity of his confession but at the same time precludes any
danger. His whole demeanor, which contrasts with but at the
same time anticipates the sinuous flattery of the fox, has the
truly impressive dignity of one who, by virtue of outward circumstance and inward conviction, has neither to disguise nor to
justify his actions.

The brutal equation of right with might is implicit in the
structure of the fable world. But the centuries-old fable maxim,
as presented by La Fontaine, is colored by the political thinking of his age. The doctrine of the divine right of kings, though
valiantly upheld by Bossuet and still officially accepted in France,
had been rudely shaken by Machiavelli, whom La Fontaine lists,
in the *Epître* to the Bishop of Soissons, as one of his favorite
authors.

La Fontaine's role as a fable writer apparently permitted him to express opinions that would have seemed treasonable in a political philosopher. The license given him is understandable, since the fable writer, unlike the political philosopher, has no need to rebuild the political edifice he is demolishing. Nor does La Fontaine show any inclination to do so. His satire of royal justice, abstracted from the general context of the fables, might lead one to see him as an incipient republican. Nothing could be further from the truth. La Fontaine is just as skeptical of the republican mystique, Vox *populi*, vox *Dei* (VIII 26), as of the royal mystique, the king can do no wrong. Had he lived a century later he would undoubtedly have enjoyed making fun of Rousseau (who smelled an enemy in La Fontaine) just as much as he enjoyed making fun of Louis XIV. In the supremely equitable fable universe what is sauce for the goose is sauce for the gander, and the doctrine of natural right no less ridiculous than the doctrine of divine right.

It so happened that the theory of natural right had not developed very far when La Fontaine wrote his fables. Yet the doctrine is vaguely adumbrated in these fables and, significantly, under the very heading that was to predominate in Locke: the natural right to property. The fable of the spider and the swallow (X 6) is a good case in point. The spider complains to Jupiter that the swallow catches numerous flies that are rightly hers, that is to say, flies that would otherwise have been caught in her web. This "insolent discourse" is of no avail; the swallow continues to snatch up all the flies she can find and finally, in one last joyful swoop, makes off with the spider web and the spider herself, trailing after.

In one sense this is merely another instance of the might-makes-right equation demonstrated in the fables about the wolf and the lion. But La Fontaine's satire is here aimed against the loser, not the winner, in what seems an extremely pertinent, though premature, criticism of the theory of property developed by Locke in his essay on civil government (1690). The spider's claim to the flies in the vicinity of her carefully woven net is based on a form of reasoning very similar to Locke's fundamental axiom: "Whatsoever, then, he removes out of the state that Nature hath provided and left it in, he hath mixed his labour with it, and joined to it something that is his own, and thereby makes it his property."

It is worth noting how often La Fontaine's fable characters resort to the all-important possessive pronoun when they are off their guard. The plaintive spider uses it four times in the space of a single, brief sentence:

"Elle me prend *mes* mouches à *ma* porte:
Miennes je puis les dire; et *mon* réseau
En serait plein sans ce maudit oiseau . . ."

"She robs me of my flies at my door:
Mine, I may say it; for my net
Would be full of them but for that cursed bird . . ."

The wolf who is planning to eat a dog refers to "his" dog (IX 10); the curate who is meditating on the payment he will receive for a funeral service refers to "his" deceased (VII 11); Pierrette counts up "her" mythical hens, pigs, cows and calves (VII 10); the miser refers to "his" money (IX 16); the bear hunters to "their" uncaught bear (V 20). As in the fable of the spider and the swallow, events always conspire to destroy the validity of the spurious possessive pronoun: the credulous wolf is put to flight by his intended victim; the predatory curate is killed by the hearse of his deceased; Pierrette's imaginary livestock vanishes into thin air when she spills her milk; the miser's treasure is stolen; and the bear hunters fail to catch their bear —in fact they are lucky to get away with their lives.

The neat anticlimaxes bear the mark of La Fontaine's Fortune, a capricious lady with a weakness for practical jokes. But

Fortune is merely acting as the agent of a more fundamental principle: no one has any "natural right" to anything. From this Olympian perspective the whole problem of conflicting property rights becomes absurd. La Fontaine has devoted a good many fables to such disputes: a wolf accuses a fox of theft (II 3); two pilgrims claim the same oyster (IX 9); a weasel appropriates a rabbit's domicile (VII 16); a pregnant bitch assumes irregular privileges (XII 8). They invariably end with an unexpected judgment from on high, equally disastrous for both parties. In no case does La Fontaine seem to be reproving the obvious miscarriage of justice: he finds the whole comedy of legal procedure, as represented by the naïve contestants as well as by the unscrupulous judge, completely meaningless.

Another element of modern democratic theory suggested and summarily disposed of by La Fontaine is the idea of the natural equality of men—or of animals. La Fontaine's apparently antiegalitarian sentiments are perfectly consistent with the point of view expressed in the fable of the elephant and Jupiter's monkey (XII 21):

> Qu'importe à ceux du firmament
> Qu'on soit mouche ou bien éléphant?

> What does it matter in the eyes of heaven
> Whether one be a fly or an elephant?

All animals are perhaps equal in the eyes of heaven; this does not mean that they are equal in practical, earthly terms. The frog is unable to blow herself up to the proportions of an ox (I 3). The crow cannot successfully impersonate the eagle (II 16); the jackdaw the peacock (IV 9); nor the donkey the lion (V 21). The small and envious rat who maintains that "we rats" are just as good as the elephants is quickly put in his place by a cat who happens to be perched on top of the elephant in question (VIII 15).

It is significant that the idea of natural equality, as expressed by La Fontaine's rat, should be linked with the idea ("we rats") of a general collectivity of rats. The lower animals, the frogs, the hens, the rodents, exist and see themselves as members of a general species. There is no class or nation of lions or foxes or wolves; the fable aristocrats exist and see themselves as individuals. This treatment—the distinct and powerful few as opposed to the undifferentiated masses—has always applied in the fable. But La Fontaine is making a different point in his fable of the rat and the elephant: group consciousness is presented not as an indication of humility but as a form of self-assertion, something that the English essayist, Arthur Clutton-Brock, has called "pooled self-esteem."

La Fontaine's rat is compensating for his relative lack of bulk by identifying himself with a general nation or class of rats, a collective entity that has a real, though indefinable, value just because it is a collective entity. However painful his recognition of the elephant's superior bulk, the rat probably feels a little better when he is intoning the ritual anthem of the rats, which has a weak rhyme but a good beat:

> "Nous ne nous prisons pas, tout petits que nous sommes,
> D'un grain moins que les éléphants."

> "We don't count ourselves, small as we are,
> At one grain less than the elephants."

La Fontaine understood the senseless word magic of the political slogan. A quick-witted bat in one of his early fables (II 5) uses it very shrewdly. Having first blundered into a mouse-hating weasel's nest, the bat insists she is a bird:

> "Je suis oiseau: voyez mes ailes.
> Vive la gent qui fend les airs!"

"I'm a bird: see my wings.
Hurray for the people who cleave the air!"

She next blunders into a bird-hating weasel's nest and protests she is a loyal rodent:

"Je suis souris: vivent les rats!
Jupiter confonde les chats!"

"I'm a mouse: hurray for the rats!
Jupiter confound the cats!"

The two hostile weasel camps, presumably, are not taken in by the bat's very imperfect resemblance to a bird or to a mouse; they are more or less hypnotized by her stirring renditions of the two antithetical anthems. Here is an instance of democratic group manipulation as effective as the fox's manipulation of the royal lion. And it undermines the moral dignity of the group ("Up with us because we are an us") just as decisively as La Fontaine in other instances undermines the moral dignity of the lion.

La Fontaine's fable politics leave little room for political beliefs of any sort. This does not mean they are devoid of moral principles. Might equals right, La Fontaine tells us in the fable of the wolf and the lamb; the very telling of the fable implies that might, however disguised by political theory, is not the same thing as right, and that the latter is a real and easily recognizable concept. It also implies that the conjunction, if only the imperfect conjunction, of might and right which must be assumed in any justifiable political system is a logical contradiction. The mere presence of material force undermines the moral idea.

There is something of the twentieth-century political purist—Péguy, Alain, Camus—in La Fontaine's general view of things, with the important difference that La Fontaine, who recognizes the necessity of material power and material force, does not aspire to the purist's Utopia. He simply views the human situation from the point of view of Jupiter's monkey or, as Spinoza would have put it, "under the form of eternity." In this he is faithful to the spirit of his age—and also to the spirit of the fable.

The Human Comedy

La Fontaine's poetic comedy merges almost imperceptibly into his social comedy. One needs only a slight change of perspective to transform the social comedy into a more general human comedy. The beasts of prey, the royal and aristocratic members of fable society, justify their privileged status with poetic fictions or shaky rationalizations. Man is so congenitally convinced of his central position in the general scheme of things that explicit arguments are hardly necessary. The assumption is simply there, rooted in his whole conception of reality, coloring his every thought and action.

In the fable of Garo and the pumpkin (IX 4) we encounter Garo, a simple-minded peasant taken from a play by Cyrano de Bergerac, in a moment of unwonted metaphysical speculation. "Why," Garo meditates, "does such a large pumpkin grow on such a tiny stem? This is extremely badly planned. If I had had any say in the matter I would have hung the pumpkin on one of those oak trees. What a shame that God never thought of asking my advice! Everything would have been so much better. That tiny acorn, no bigger than my little finger, is suspended on the oak. God must have made a mistake."

Highly pleased with himself and apparently exhausted by these mental exertions, Garo falls asleep under the oak in question. An acorn falls on his face and he awakens with a bloody nose. "Oh, oh!" he cries. "And supposing it had been a pumpkin!

God never would have wanted *that* to happen. Now I understand!"

The fable's opening verse "Dieu fait bien ce qu'il fait" (God
knows what he is doing), like Polonius's "to thine own self be
true," is often taken at face value as a profound reflection of the
philosopher poet. Unwary readers, forgetting that they are being
harangued, not by La Fontaine, not by Shakespeare, but by a
semi-imbecile peasant or a senile pedant, are all too willing to
bask in the reassuring warmth of a moral truism. Garo's ap-
proval of the divine workmanship is hardly less ridiculous than
his previous criticisms. The whole point of the fable is the absurdity of the common assumption God has, or at any rate ought
to have, created the universe according to man's own highly limited notions of law and order.

Here is the principal key to La Fontaine's wolf: this would-be
moralist, this would-be rationalist, so manifestly incapable of
adapting himself to an environment, including his own animal
instincts, that is based on neither rational nor moral principles.
His naïve and well-intentioned egoism would disarm the most
indignant moralist. What is particularly touching about La Fontaine's wolf is his unshakable conviction that all other forms of
life will naturally, and of their own accord, adapt themselves
to his personal interests and preconceptions. This is what makes
him such an easy victim and such an unsuccessful hunter.

He sincerely believes, for example, that by simply adopting a
shepherd's hat and crook, and thus announcing his intended disguise as a shepherd, he will become indistinguishable from a real
shepherd (III 3).

Il aurait volontiers écrit sur son chapeau:
"C'est moi qui suis Guillot, berger de ce troupeau."

He would have been perfectly capable of writing on his hat:
"It is I who am Guillot, the shepherd of this flock."

Like a small child who announces that he is hiding behind a tree, the wolf apparently imagines that his supposed antagonists, the sheep, will have the grace to co-operate with his deception.

When an angry mother threatens to give her naughty child to the wolf, the wolf naturally takes her at her word and stands by in happy anticipation of the treat. The mother, seeing that her threat has failed to produce the desired effect, tells the child not to cry; they will kill the wolf if he comes to their house. The wolf is not only outraged by this betrayal; his tender sensibilities are deeply wounded (IV 16).

> "Qu'est ceci? s'écria le mangeur de moutons.
> Dire d'un, puis d'un autre? Est-ce ainsi que l'on traite
> Les gens faits comme moi? Me prend-on pour un sot?"

> "What's this?" the sheep-eater exclaimed to himself.
> "Say one thing, then the other? Is this a way to treat
> People of my sort? Do they take me for a fool?"

On another occasion the wolf encounters a dog and prepares to carry him off for his dinner (IX 10). The dog objects that he does not, at present, constitute a fitting meal for the wolf. "Let me go home and fatten up a bit first." The wolf finds his argument entirely plausible and entertains not the slightest suspicion that his intended victim might conceivably prefer to escape destruction. Not only does he believe the dog; he lets him go and then, to crown it all, returns to see if the dog has put on any weight—a striking crescendo of credulity that La Fontaine expresses, in a perfectly neutral tone of voice, by one of his repeated-syntax, expanded-verse-length constructions:

> Le loup le croit, le loup le laisse;
> Le loup quelques jours écoulés
> Revient voir si son chien n'est point meilleur à prendre.

The wolf believes him, the wolf lets him go;
The wolf after a few days have gone by
Returns to see if his dog is not a better catch.

The dog, now safe on his own grounds, tells the wolf that he and his friend, an enormous watchdog, will be right out.

"Ce loup," La Fontaine comments, "ne savait pas encor bien son métier" (this wolf had not yet learned his trade very well). Unlike the other animal characters, all expert members of their particular species, the wolf never really adjusts to the problem of being a wolf. Standing midway between the sublime vacuity of the lion and the enlightened cynicism of the fox, he either thinks too much or else not enough and is thus constantly tripped up by his own rudimentary logic.

The wolf is the one fable animal to show the faint beginnings of a moral conscience. Here again La Fontaine seems to have grasped the buried fable intuition of an actual fact of animal life. According to Lorenz, the wolf, because he can hunt successfully only in numbers, is a highly socialized animal equipped with a number of built-in inhibitions. A wolf, for example, cannot bring himself to kill another wolf who has technically surrendered by offering his jugular vein to his antagonist. "You can see that he would like to," Lorenz writes, "but he just cannot!"

La Fontaine's wolf maintains an almost pedantic regard for truth, although this is most apparent in his indignant appraisal of the various ruses of his antagonists. He would like to be able to prove that his own behavior is correct and, as in his encounter with the lamb, becomes extremely ferocious when he is unable to do so. He would also like to be liked—an unfortunate weakness in a carnivore.

In one of La Fontaine's later fables (X 5) the wolf even tries to reform. A highly humanitarian wolf one day began to reflect upon his evil reputation. "Almost everyone," he said to himself, "seems to hate me; dogs, hunters, villagers, they are all against me. No sooner does a child cry than its mother threatens it with the wolf. And all this for a skimpy donkey, a rotten sheep, a peevish dog. Very well. I will no longer eat living things; I'll munch grass, put myself out to graze; die of hunger if necessary; is that such a cruel fate?"

These sentiments have an undeniable grandeur, particularly as the wolf concludes by paraphrasing the last words of Aeneas' noble enemy Turnus (*Aeneid* XII 646), a verse La Fontaine had previously rendered for Pintrel's translation of Seneca's *Epistles*: "Est-ce un si grand malheur de mourir?" (Is it so terrible to die?)

Just as he is saying these words the wolf happens to see a group of shepherds roasting a lamb. His indignant reaction, motivated by his fear of ridicule as well as by his sense of justice, is characteristic: Oh! oh! Here am *I* feeling guilty about eating sheep while the sheeps' guardians, they and their dogs, are stuffing themselves!

> "Et moi loup j'en ferai scrupule?
> Non, par tous les dieux non. Je serais ridicule."

> "And I, a wolf, shall have scruples about it?
> No, by all the gods no. I would look ridiculous."

La Fontaine's wolf has a striking three-dimensional reality about him. This is because he is the character who is seen from the inside. And La Fontaine explores every corner of the inner landscape—an absurdly vulnerable conjunction of vanity and self-delusion and good intentions—with the assurance of one who is on his own ground. As often happens with a character who is seen from the inside, there is a good deal of La Fontaine in La Fontaine's wolf.

La Fontaine too was a self-confessed dupe, all too ready to swallow any attractive bait and rush headlong into the delightful fairy-tale land of wishful thinking (VII 10) where

Tout le bien du monde est à nous,
Tous les honneurs, toutes les femmes.

All the wealth in the world is ours,
All the honors, all the women.

Don't laugh at the credulous wolf who jumps into a well in pursuit of a nonexistent cheese, he warns. We are all constantly doing exactly the same sort of thing.

La Fontaine had good reason to know. To begin with, he had an unfortunate tendency to fall head over heels in love with almost any young woman who gave him half a chance. As he himself observed in a letter explaining his previous passion for Claudine, the vulgar and designing wife of the poet Colletet: "Don't you know that when I am in love I no more see people's faults than a mole a hundred feet underground?"

La Fontaine was also blinded, on occasion, by his urgent desire for both immediate popularity and lasting fame. Just as the wolf took the angry mother at her word when she promised to give him her naughty baby, La Fontaine believed that Lully was really willing to drop his customary librettist, Quinault, for La Fontaine. He spent four months writing an insipid pastoral opera, *Daphné*, only to discover that Lully had never really intended to collaborate with La Fontaine and had all the time been working on another opera with Quinault. As La Fontaine explains:

A tort, à droit, me demanda
Du doux, du tendre, et semblables sornettes,
    Petits mots, jargons d'amourettes
Confits au miel; bref, il m'enquinauda.

Win or lose, he asked me for
Sweetness and light, and suchlike rubbish,
    Baby words, lovey-dovey talk
Preserved in honey; in short, he made me look like a fool.

La Fontaine's "enquinauda," which is taken from the adjective "quinaud," abashed or foolish, involves a pun on the name of the ultra-flowery Quinault.

As with the wolf, the inevitable awakening and painful recognition—I must look like a terrible fool—gives rise to high indignation, an indignation vented in bitter satires and epigrams against the Claudines and Lullys of this world who so abuse him. La Fontaine's diatribe against Lully compares him to a voracious wolf. Anyone familiar with La Fontaine's fables will recognize La Fontaine's version of the Lully-La Fontaine incident as one of his many fables about the fox and the wolf, with the clever Italian cast as fox and La Fontaine himself as wolf.

La Fontaine, like his wolf, was sometimes incommoded by an uneasy conscience. He seems to have tried, not very often or very seriously perhaps, to live a more regulated life. He was never able to keep his good resolutions.

The obvious distinction between La Fontaine and his wolf is that La Fontaine was able to create the wolf; in other words, self-knowledge. It is self-knowledge of a rather special kind: not the ability to spot one's own distinctive quirks and humors that is often a form of self-flattery, but the ability to recognize the great unacknowledged contradictions of human character as they appear in one's own inner self. La Fontaine's "I" is merely a more specific and intimate instance of his all-inclusive "everybody."

The wolf, in whom La Fontaine invested so great a knowledge of himself, has the same universality. La Fontaine's other fable characters, the lion, the fox, the donkey, incorporate certain traits of human character. His wolf, this sinner, penitent and everlasting dupe, incorporates the fundamental predicament of man himself —that other species which, as La Fontaine observed of his wolf, has somehow failed to master its particular profession.

La Fontaine's fables, in so far as they develop into a "human comedy," thus raise a number of general human problems, problems that had been previously raised in Montaigne's *Apologie de Raimond Sebond*. La Fontaine was presumably familiar with this work, a bold, although veiled, attack on the scholastic assumption that the ultimate nature of the universe is consonant with and may be apprehended by the laws of human reason.

"What, for example," Montaigne observes, "is more futile than to try to divine God by our analogies and conjectures, to regulate him and the world according to our capacity and our laws?" Is this not a fairly accurate analysis of La Fontaine's peasant-philosopher Garo?

Here is the conclusion of La Fontaine's fable on moderation (IX 11): "animals are much better disciplined than we are and contain themselves with greater moderation behind the limits that nature has prescribed."

Here is the point of view established by Jupiter's monkey (XII 21): "As if it were any more or less (for God) to shake an empire or the leaf on a tree, and as if his providence acted differently, determining the outcome of a battle or the hop of a flea!"

La Fontaine's wolf exemplifies the fundamental issue raised in Montaigne's *Apologie:* "It is conceivable that there are natural laws (for men), as can be seen with other creatures; but with us they have been lost, this fine human reason everywhere taking upon itself to dominate and to command, blurring and confusing the face of things in accordance with its vanity and inconsistency." In other words: this faculty of human reason, which separates us from the natural order without at the same time furnishing an alternative guide to existence, is it so much of an advantage as we generally suppose? and are men, by virtue of their reason, so much better off than animals?

It was not a very prudent question in La Fontaine's day. The libertine poet Théophile's outspoken espousal of the Montaigne "heresy"—animals are probably better off than we are—had led to his imprisonment, very nearly his death, in 1623. As the prosecutor, Molé, asked in his projected interrogation: Did he not insidiously encourage "contempt for man and praise for beasts who follow nature"? La Fontaine, understandably enough, approaches the inflammatory issue with caution. But it is clear that he does approach it in his last four books of fables.

In the fable of the wolf and the shepherds, for example, the wolf has a somewhat ambiguous role as both an ironic image of man and an indignant judge of man. We are invited to forgive the wolf (and humanity in general) for its carnivorous appetites but to accept the wolf's denunciation of the shepherds (and humanity in general) for their hypocritical denial as well as their unbridled indulgence of these appetites.

In one of his last fables (XII 1) La Fontaine describes Ulysses' unsuccessful attempts to persuade his companions, fallen under Circe's enchantment, to resume their human shapes. La Fontaine, who dedicated the fable to the young Duc de Bourgogne, at that time heir apparent, appears to condemn their behavior. Like Montaigne, who also used this anecdote, he never even attempts to refute the arguments put forward in favor of animal, as opposed to human, existence. "You call me a beast of prey," declares the wolf. "But you who are talking, what are you? If I were a man would I be any less bloodthirsty? Not only do you devour sheep, as I do. Sometimes, for a mere word, you all strangle each other. Are men [and the wolf is here quoting La Rochefoucauld and Hobbes] not wolves for each other?"

As in the fable of the wolf and the shepherds, La Fontaine is covertly attacking the anthropocentric premises of fable symbolism: the manifest absurdity of the human use of the wolf as a symbol of cruelty. The same point is carried even further in the fable of the man and the serpent (X 1), La Fontaine's most famous and most serious indictment of man. A man finds a serpent which he prepares to destroy because it is a symbol of ingratitude. The serpent replies that man, not the serpent, is the real symbol of ingratitude. The man, anxious to prove that he is right, agrees to submit the argument to three witnesses, a cow, an ox, and a fruit tree. Each witness points out how, after a lifetime of devoted service to man, he or she is neglected or abused and thus decides in favor of the serpent. The man, like the wolf in the fable of the wolf and the lamb, angrily dismisses these inconvenient arguments and summarily kills the serpent.

The fable, taken from the Indian fable writer Pilpay, reflects a somewhat Oriental "respect for life" which, to Western eyes, might seem to verge on sentimentality. And in the nuclear age an old cow, an old ox, and an old fruit tree may seem trivial witnesses. These, however, are the age-old symbols of Nature in her role as protector and sustainer of human life, a point of view La Fontaine carried over in his treatment of the fable. The rich, slow-moving language of the cow and the ox is built on the beneficent rhythms of natural existence, a melody that culminates in La Fontaine's final elegy to the fruit tree:

> Il servait de refuge
> Contre le chaud, la pluie, et la fureur des vents;
> Pour nous seuls il ornait les jardins et les champs.
> L'ombrage n'était pas le seul bien qu'il sût faire;
> Il courbait sous les fruits; cependant, pour salaire,
> Un rustre l'abattait, c'était là son loyer,
> Quoique pendant tout l'an libéral il nous donne
> Ou des fleurs au printemps, ou du fruit en automne;
> L'ombre l'été; l'hiver, les plaisirs du foyer.

> It served as a refuge
> Against heat, the rain, and the rage of the winds;
> Just for us it brightened the gardens and fields.
> Shade was not the only gift it could make;
> It bent under its fruits; and yet, as a salary,
> A boor chopped it down, that was its pay,
> Though throughout the whole liberal year it had given
> Either flowers in spring, or fruit in autumn;
> Shade in summer; in winter, the pleasures of the hearth.

This passage, with its gentle, whispering sound patterns, its smooth but shifting cadences, translates the very essence of tree-hood. The leaves and branches, rustling and swaying in the wind, are singing their song of seasonal change and plenitude. How harshly does the rasping prose of Eliot's "human voices" wake us as the man, tone deaf to the persuasive music of the tree, breaks in:

"Je suis bien bon, dit-il, d'écouter ces gens-là."

"Why am I listening to these characters?" he said.

And the arbitrary execution of the serpent is a fitting symbol of man's wanton disruption of the natural order on which he, like every other living thing, depends. It has the same element of sacrilege that Coleridge saw in the Ancient Mariner's shooting of the albatross.

La Fontaine hides the moral, so far removed from conventional fable morality, in the context of the fable and pretends that he is illustrating the same practical truth underlined in so many of the early fables: might makes right. The hidden judgment nonetheless prevails. The comedy has turned into a potential tragedy —a tragedy relieved by La Fontaine's underlying conviction that we are not really so distinct from nature as we appear to be. In the fable of the wolf and the lamb La Fontaine assumes that the reader, unlike the wolf, can distinguish might from right; in the fable of the man and the serpent he assumes that the reader, unlike the man in the fable, can understand the language of the tree.

IV

The Fable as Poetry

Words and Actions

La Fontaine's use of animal characters to satirize specifically human activities—poetry, social organization, political theory, theology—is as much as to say: my animals are not really animals at all. At the same time, the whole object of the comedy is to expose the unreality of these specifically human activities. The real fiction in a La Fontaine fable is not the convention of the speaking animal; it is the convention of human speech.

This is a typically late-Renaissance attitude, speech being equated with the unreal paper universe of scholasticism. Marlowe gives Faust's desire "to deal not in empty words but deeds" as an important reason for his pact with the devil. There is also a much older, peasantlike distrust of speech current in proverbs and folk sayings the world over. *Le Roman de Renart* is full of of them: "words cost nothing"; "there is a long way between saying and doing"; "one should not speak with one's mouth full, as Cato wisely taught his son." The fable of the fox and the crow is a good illustration of Cato's alleged advice to his son; but aside from specific instances like this the fable form is so constructed as to expose the unreality of verbal speech. Words are no more than a superficial veil, half-disguising, half-betraying the actual shape of reality, which is always an action or an event.

This active quality is one of the great virtues of the fable form, particularly as compared to other popular seventeenth-century forms like the ode, the elegy and the epistle. Good seventeenth-

century lyric poets like Saint-Amant and Théophile, though recently rediscovered and republished, are not widely read. For
all their enthusiasm and intensity they fail to carry the reader
along with them. Verse follows verse, and stanza stanza, in an
aimless, haphazard way without any thought of structural organization. "Oh, how I love Solitude!" Saint-Amant cries. For
the first three or four stanzas one is quite happy to abandon
oneself to the sheer lyric beauty of his rhapsody. By the twentieth
stanza one is inclined to ask: so what?

La Fontaine's fables, like Molière's comedies and Racine's
tragedies, have a definite form: form is the structure of an action.
In La Fontaine's early fables the action is direct and explicit;
yet even in the later ones, where plot is sometimes subordi-
nated to speculative or lyric meditations, La Fontaine retains this
sense of dramatic structure. An idea, an emotion, a general consideration of any sort, is presented as an action or a drama. This
is one of the reasons for his frequent use of the first person in
these later fables. The "je" transforms the abstract generalization
into a concrete event, whether this be a daydream, as in the
fable about the milkmaid (VII 10), or, as in another fable (VII
18), a discussion of perception:

Quand l'eau courbe un bâton, ma raison le redresse . . .

When water bends a stick, my reason straightens it . . .

In the Aesopian fable the action is no more than a plot: a good
plot, to be sure, but a bare skeleton structure showing the interaction of abstract, mechanical forces. The crow opens his mouth
and the cheese falls to the ground; the long-beaked stork cannot eat from a flat plate; the rigid tree is uprooted by the hur-
ricane. It remained for La Fontaine to transform the abstract
motions into animate rhythms.

"Cela est peint!" . . . it's painted! Thus, in a letter (1671) to

her daughter, Madame de Sévigné described her enthusiastic reaction to one of La Fontaine's fables. The adjective has stuck
ever since. This is nonetheless a singularly inappropriate definition of La Fontaine's fable poetry—a poetry so bare of plastic
description, or imagery, or color. One might, with some justification, apply the word "painted" to the poetry of La Fontaine's predecessors—Régnier, Saint-Amant and Théophile—which
abounds with verbal portraits, landscapes, and interiors. One might
also apply it to certain passages of La Fontaine's *Songe de
Vaux*. But even though the poem was commissioned as a verbal
description of Fouquet's new establishment, La Fontaine, by
choosing to write his description in the form of a dream, avoided
his appointed task as far as possible.

It is true that analogies between painting and poetry were just
beginning to become fashionable in La Fontaine's day, a form
of aesthetic theory that was to run riot in the eighteenth century.
There are a number of such analogies in La Fontaine's poetry,
but generally emphasizing the disparity rather than the similarity
of the two mediums. In the second section of *Le Songe de Vaux*
the four fairies of architecture, painting, gardening, and poetry
(apparently listed in the inverse order of La Fontaine's preference)
dispute their respective merits. Calliopée, the poetry fairy, points
out that while painting can only represent corporeal bodies,
poetry can convey the intangible movements of the soul:

"Il n'appartient qu'à moi de montrer les ressorts
Qui font mouvoir une âme, et la rendent visible;
Seule j'expose aux sens ce qui n'est pas sensible,"

"I alone am empowered to show the springs
That move the soul, and make it visible;
I alone reveal to the senses that which is not perceptible."

La Fontaine's play on the double meaning of the word "move,"
as referring to both physical motions and inner emotions, is sig-

nificant. It is as a movement, or rhythm, that the invisible is made visible in poetry—and in poetry alone. La Fontaine is already pointing out, as Lessing was to do a century later, that while painting, a spatial medium, expresses forms directly but motions only indirectly, poetry, a temporal medium, expresses motions directly but forms only indirectly. The observation throws a certain amount of light on the weakness of La Fontaine's contes both as erotic suggestion and as poetry. As La Fontaine explains in *Le Tableau*, the conte is a veiled picture: an attempt to portray indecent objects without using any indecent words. The "veil" is necessary because the names of certain objects are more indecent than painted representations of these objects. The problem of decent indecency, which is actually the whole point of this particular genre, is more easily solved than the problem of verbal portraiture. At the end of the story La Fontaine admits that he has failed:

> Les mots et les couleurs ne sont choses pareilles;
>   Ni les yeux ne sont les oreilles.

> Words and colors are not the same things;
>   And eyes are not ears.

La Fontaine's fable poetry, to remain within the somewhat dubious realm of aesthetic analogy, is far closer to the art of the mime—part clown, part actor, and part dancer. Animal and human characters are created not as corporeal entities but as voices, gestures, attitudes. This is particularly obvious in the sobriquets La Fontaine invents for his various animal characters: "La gent trotte-menu" (III 18), the small-trotting people; "Le chat grippe-fromage . . . Ronge-maille le rat" (VIII 22), the cat grab-the-cheese and gnaw-the-net the rat; "Le mangeur de moutons" (IV 16), the sheep-eater. La Fontaine's descriptive passages are based on the same general principle, here supported by

his metrical constructions. A family of baby larks leaves its nest
(IV 22):

> Et les petits en même temps,
> Voletants, se culebutants,
> Délogèrent tous sans trompette.

> And the little ones all together,
> Fluttering, tumbling head over heels,
> All surreptitiously decamped.

The iron pot and the earthenware pot set out for a walk together
in a precarious seven-syllable meter, a verse rarely used in La
Fontaine's day (V 2):

> Mes gens s'en vont à trois pieds,
> Clopin clopant, comme ils peuvent,
> L'un contre l'autre jetés,
> Au moindre hoquet qu'ils treuvent.

> My friends start off on three legs,
> Bumpety bump, however they can,
> The one thrown against the other,
> At every slightest jolt encountered.

The tortoise races with the hare (VI 10):

> Elle part, elle s'évertue;
> Elle se hâte avec lenteur.

> She starts off, she tries hard;
> She hurries slowly.

All these different forms of being, created not as shapes but
as movements, convey a certain physical sensation of existence;
they also convey an equivalent state of mind: the eager impa-

tience of unco-ordinated muscular energy; the terror of imbalance; uninspired, methodical exertion.

In La Fontaine's later fables these comically pedestrian gaits and mental attitudes turn into something that is very close to dancing. A young rabbit pays homage to the rising sun and then goes home (VII 16):

> Après qu'il eut brouté, trotté, fait tous ses tours,
> Janot Lapin retourne aux souterrains séjours.

> After he'd nibbled, trotted, done all his tricks,
> Janot Lapin returns to the underground realm.

A swallow, chasing flies, darts and twists in her flight (X 6):

> Caracolant, frisant l'air et les eaux . . .

> Caracoling, skimming the air and the waters . . .

A fox, by moonlight, fascinates three sleepy turkeys (XII 18):

> Arlequin n'eût exécuté
> Tant de différents personnages.
> Il élevait sa queue, il la faisait briller,
> Et cent mille autres badinages . . .

> Harlequin could not have mimed
> So many different characters.
> He raised his tail, he made it glitter,
> And a thousand other sprightly tricks . . .

As Yeats has asked: "How can we know the dancer from the dance?" These perfectly co-ordinated natural athletes are enjoying, each in his different realm, the luxury of pure physical wellbeing.

By thus reintegrating physical and moral existence in the sub-stratum of rhythmic motion La Fontaine brings the fable met-aphor to life. The fable of Death and the woodsman, for ex-ample, is based on a familiar figure of speech: life is a heavy burden. Aesop, whom La Fontaine follows closely, put the figure in a dramatic form. A poverty-stricken old woodsman is strug-gling home with his burden of firewood. At length exhausted, and despairing of his lot, he puts down his firewood and calls for Death. Death comes immediately and asks: "Why did you call me?" "To help me load up my firewood again," replies the woodsman.

The woodsman, struggling homeward, is bent under the com-bined weight of his firewood and his poverty-stricken old age. His provisional abandonment of his firewood parallels his con-templated abandonment of life. His explanation of his appeal to Death—I called you to help me load up my wood again—paral-lels his simultaneous resumption of life. What is missing in Aesop and what La Fontaine has supplied in his fable (I 16) is a poetic synthesis of the two terms of the metaphor: an effec-tive demonstration of the tremendous difficulty, under certain circumstances, of simply continuing to carry a heavy load—or to exist.

Un pauvre bûcheron, tout couvert de ramée,
Sous le faix du fagot aussi bien que des ans
Gémissant et courbé marchait à pas pesants,
Et tâchait de gagner sa chaumine enfumée.

A poor woodsman, all covered with branches,
Weighed down with firewood as well as with years
Groaning and bent walked with heavy steps,
And tried to reach his smoky cottage.

The effect of painful exertion is partly due to the grammat-ical structure of the sentence. One would be tempted to use the passive tense or an adjectival phrase in describing a situation of this kind: his forward progress *was impeded* by the weight of his burden; he was so heavily *burdened* that he had to walk very slowly. La Fontaine uses active verbs: "marchait," "tâchait." The composite burden of old age and firewood is thus actively conveyed in the woodsman's forward struggle against the downward pull of gravity and despair. The effect is well articulated by the general movement of the passage: the heavy, closely juxtaposed alliterations (*f*aix, *f*agot; *p*as *p*esants); the emphatic internal rhymes (bûchero*n*, a*ns*, gémiss*ant*, pes*ants*; ram*ée*, f*aix*, courb*é*, march*ait*, tâch*ait*, gagn*er*, enfum*ée*); the long and closely integrated sentence which seems to be struggling against the natural rhythm of the alexandrin.

La Fontaine's punctuation, because it is often governed by rhythmic rather than grammatical considerations, sometimes seems a bit haphazard. The omission of the comma at the end of the second verse and at the caesura of the third verse is undoubtedly deliberate. This is the blind, hopeless, one step after the other progression of a man who is at the end of his physical and moral resources. If he stopped going, even for an instant, he might never have the courage to start again.

Boileau put the same fable in verse form, thus inadvisedly inviting comparison with La Fontaine:

Le dos chargé de bois, et le corps tout en eau,
Un pauvre bûcheron, dans l'extrême vieillesse,
Marchait en haletant de peine et de détresse.

His back laden with wood, his body dripping,
A poor woodsman, in extreme old age,
Walked panting with effort and distress.

Boileau, apparently, has failed to perceive the basic metaphor of the fable, underlined in the second verse of La Fontaine's poem: "weighed down with firewood as well as with years." Small wonder that he should fail to articulate the metaphor. La Fontaine conveys old age and despair as a physical and moral reality; Boileau simply tells us that his woodsman is old, that he is distressed. His sharply cut alexandrins progress smoothly, even jauntily—a metrical incongruity that would be less obvious had La Fontaine not shown us how the woodsman really walked.

One might say that the physical movements of La Fontaine's fable characters, since these correspond to inner states of mind, are actually a form of speech. The same principle works in reverse. Speech itself, not as rational discourse but as the reflection of an inner state of mind, is a physical movement. These movements are apparent in the different intonations of La Fontaine's fable characters. With the fable of the animals stricken by the plague there are contrasting rhythms in the lion's plain statement of fact, the fox's sinuous flattery, the plodding confession of the donkey—rhythms that correspond to the animals' respective gaits. The rhythm, or movement, of a speech often helps to determine its meaning and, conversely, the meaning helps to indicate the movement. The latter is particularly true with static forms like the oak in the fable of the oak and the reed (I 22):

Cependant que mon front, au Caucase pareil,
Non content d'arrêter les rayons du soleil,
    Brave l'effort de la tempête.

Whereas my brow, rivaling the Caucasus,
Not content to stop the rays of the sun,
    Defies the straining tempest.

The proud and hyperbolic language of the tree expresses an arrogant upward and outward thrust.

Sometimes, as with the lion's confession, an animal's way of speaking contrasts ironically with the meaning of his speech. Sometimes, as with the lion's final argument in support of his claim to the entire stag, the meaning is completely supplanted by the physical movement of the speech. The intricate legal controversy of the wolf and the fox (II 3) seems to boil down to a question of pure lung power:

> Après qu'on eut bien contesté,
> Répliqué, crié, tempêté . . .

> After considerable contesting,
> Countering, shouting, thundering . . .

This reduction of speech to physical action is more subtly conveyed in La Fontaine's later fables. The physical and moral characters of the magpie who has been invited to entertain a condescending eagle (XII 11) merge indistinguishably in a spastic, hippety-hoppety state of being:

> Caquet-bon bec alors de jaser au plus dru
> Sur ceci, sur cela, sur tout. L'homme d'Horace
> Disant le bien, le mal, à travers champs, n'eût su
> Ce qu'en fait de babil y savait notre agasse.
> Elle offre d'avertir de tout ce qui se passe,
> > Sautant, allant de place en place,
> Bon espion, Dieu sait.

> So Cackle-good beak starts chattering nineteen to the dozen
> About this, about that, about everything. The man in Horace
> Speaking good and evil, across country, would not have known
> As much about gossip as our magpie knew.
> She offers to report on everything that is happening,
> > Jumping, moving from place to place,
> A good spy, God knows.

The effect, as regards both the magpie's conversation and her gait, depends, among other things, on La Fontaine's accumulation of rapid antitheses—*sur ceci, sur cela; le bien, le mal; de place en place.* He uses the same device in his description of a hard-to-please young girl who criticizes all her suitors (VII 5):

> L'un n'avait en l'esprit nulle délicatesse;
> L'autre avait le nez fait de cette façon-là;
> C'était ceci, c'était cela,
> C'était tout . . .

> The one had no delicacy of mind;
> The other had that kind of a nose;
> It was this, it was that,
> It was everything . . .

And he also uses it in his description, or nightmare, of an argumentative wife (VII 2):

> Rien ne la contentait, rien n'était comme il faut:
> On se levait trop tard, on se couchait trop tôt;
> Puis du blanc, puis du noir, puis encore autre chose.

> Nothing could please her, nothing was right:
> They got up too late, they retired too early;
> Then it's white, then it's black, then it's still something else.

A French movie on the subject of bores (the very theme of the Horace satire mentioned in the fable of the magpie and the eagle) hit on the idea of photographing the mouth of an interminable talker and at the same time cutting the sound track. This is more or less what La Fontaine has done. The actual content of the tirade is indefinite (nothing) or trivial (hours of rising and retiring) or, at the end, completely meaningless (white and black). The only thing that matters is the relentless up-and-down, up-and-down movement of the woman's jaws.

The speech no less than the physical behavior of La Fontaine's fable characters reveals something that the French philosopher Alain has called "the human animal": the fundamental structure of a personality as revealed in its unconscious movements. Words can lie, and facial grimaces and bodily gestures too; but the intimate rhythms of our being that determine the *way* we talk or smile or gesticulate are always true. The most shameless hypocrites of La Fontaine's fable population—the fox, the cat—are actually as candid, as ingenuous, as their victims— the wolf, the sow. Truth is implicit in the very nature of the fable universe.

This cutting of the sound track of human speech is more than a purely satirical device conducive to counterpoetry. Claudel has provided another analogy which perhaps brings us a little closer to the spirit of La Fontaine's fables. "Suppose our delicate fancier [of the French language] . . . should, for example, hear two ladies from the provinces or Paris talking behind a wall in such a way that he has no difficulty in leaving the meaning on the other side of the screen and only the music reaches him. In what fresh and unexpected patterns will this *visible speech* inscribe itself before his eyes! What a dialogue between these voices! What originality and vigor in the attacks! What ever-changing cadences! What divisions of the verses! What harmonies between the tonalities, more delicious than the harmony of red and gray! What elegant undulations of the sentence, punctuated without any regard for grammar and terminating in the cry of a warbler!"

The passage so well, though inadvertently, conveys the specific charm of La Fontaine's fable poetry: a crystallization of the unconscious, and generally undetected, harmonies of everyday discourse in recognizable aesthetic patterns. It would appear that La Fontaine himself was familiar with Claudel's mechanism of an imaginary screen. Half-asleep at a dinner party or a séance of the French Academy, abstracted, inattentive, he was perhaps listening to the underlying pattern of a conversation as he might listen to the sound of running water or the wind in the trees. He could then change the pattern, so much more captivating and instructive than the conversation itself, into an appropriate verbal equivalent.

When La Fontaine is translating the language of plants and animals, the screen is no longer necessary. The problem here is to discover, by some process of internal imitation, the exact human equivalent for each characteristic gesture, movement, attitude, much as Proust's narrator, confronted by the enigma of the hawthorn blossoms, attempted to imitate the "gesture of their efflorescence" in his inmost being.

La Fontaine's conception of speech, both animal and human, as a rhythmic motion expressing an unconscious, inner state of being comes fairly close to the borderline of abstract poetry. In a few instances La Fontaine crosses the line:

Puis du blanc, puis du noir, puis encore autre chose.

The elimination of the surface meaning, Claudel's imaginary screen, allows us to hear the sound of a sentence as a thing in itself, just as the absence of subject in an abstract painting allows us to see forms and colors as things in themselves. With La Fontaine this is not a conscious or arbitrary mannerism; it is imposed by the nature of his subject, the fable convention of the speaking animal.

In the early fables, still characterized as "Aesop's lies," La Fontaine does not always take his speaking animals very seriously. He will sometimes deliberately draw attention to the artificiality of the convention: the frog approaches the rat and "speaks in her language" (IV 11); the little carp speaks to the fisherman "in his fashion" (V 3); the discontented donkey "complains in his patois" (III 1); the fox addresses the crow "more or less in these terms" (I 2). We are not very far removed from the highly transparent fiction of the speaking salmon in one of the incidents of *Le Songe de Vaux*.

La Fontaine is here catering to the tastes of his immediate public. The fiction of the speaking animal was then popular in literary parlor games, the various participants taking the names of different animals. Voiture's famous "letter from the carp to the pike," written to the Duc d'Enghien after the latter had crossed the Rhine, refers to an occasion in the Rambouillet salon when the two men had taken the names of these two fishes.

Voiture's letter, though it now seems a somewhat labored form of badinage, was much admired at the time and apparently familiar to La Fontaine. The fox's salutation of the crow, "Hé bonjour, Monsieur du Corbeau" is reminiscent of the carp's greeting to the pike, "Eh! bonjour, mon compère le Brochet." And La Fontaine, here deliberately alluding to Voiture's letter, introduces "mon compère le Brochet" into the fable of the fastidious heron (VII 4).

The fishly oath of Voiture's carp, "tête d'un poisson" (by the head of a fish), resembles the various animal oaths of La Fontaine's early fables. La Fontaine will sometimes give an ironic twist to an existing expression by attributing it to an appropriate animal character. The old-fashioned ejaculation "par ma barbe" (by my beard), which no doubt fell into disuse when beards were no longer fashionable, is, for example, put into the mouth of a goat (III 5). Sometimes La Fontaine adapts an existing oath to his various animal characters, his numerous variations on the expression "ma foi," or upon my word, being based on the latter principle: on my word as an animal; on my word as a lion; on my word as an owl.

Yet even in the early fables La Fontaine's animal language cannot be properly characterized by verbal devices of the kind. In the introductory verses of the second book of fables La Fontaine claims that he has invented a "new language" that enables animals, even plants and trees, to become speaking creatures:

> Cependant jusqu'ici d'un langage nouveau
> J'ai fait parler le loup et répondre l'agneau;
> J'ai passé plus avant: les arbres et les plantes
> Sont devenus chez moi créatures parlantes.
> Qui ne prendrait ceci pour un enchantement?

> Nonetheless thus far in a new language
> I've made the wolf talk and the lamb reply;
> I have gone even further: trees and plants
> Have become, with me, speaking creatures.
> Who would not take this for an enchantment?

La Fontaine here sees himself in the role of a ventriloquist, inventing an appropriate language for animals and plants; he does not yet go so far as to say there is an actual language of animals and plants that he has translated in his fables. This claim, as it appears some ten years later in the "Epilogue" to the eleventh book of fables, constitutes La Fontaine's final, and retrospective, definition of his fable poetry:

> C'est ainsi que ma muse, aux bords d'une onde pure,
>   Traduisait en langue des dieux
>   Tout ce que disent sous les cieux
> Tant d'êtres empruntant la voix de la nature.
>   Truchement de peuples divers,
> Je les faisais servir d'acteurs en mon ouvrage:
>   Car tout parle dans l'univers;
>   Il n'est rien qui n'ait son langage.

> Thus my muse, by a limpid stream,
>   Translated into the language of the gods
>   Everything said under the skies
> By so many beings borrowing the voice of nature.

Interpreter for diverse peoples,
I used them as actors in my work:
   For everything speaks in the universe;
   Nothing there is without its language.

La Fontaine's later conception of himself as an interpreter, translating the voice of nature as this is expressed by all living things, is no mere figure of speech. It corresponds to his later conviction that there is a real, not merely a conventional or imaginary, link between the human mind and the natural universe of which it is a part.

The Voice of Nature

In 1673 La Fontaine, then fifty-two years old and without any means of support, had the good fortune to find a friend in Madame de La Sablière, who took him into her household. He was to stay on until her death twenty years later. A lively and cultivated woman, Madame de La Sablière attracted intellectual as well as social lions to her circle: mathematicians, physicians, astronomers, philosophers. The conversational tone, according to La Fontaine, was gay and varied and considerably freer than that prevailing in other salons of the time.

The new intellectual stimulus shows through in the fables published in 1678 and 1679 (Books VII-XI). In the early fables La Fontaine had countered the conventional poetic myth of man the demigod with the fable myth of man the animal. In the later fables he is concerned with a new and more formidable antagonist: Descartes's myth of man half-god and half-machine. Descartes's philosophy was not, however, presented as a myth. It posed, and purported to answer, the fundamental riddle of reality: what is mind? what is matter? what is the relation of the one to the other? It was inevitable that La Fontaine, when he came to consider, and ultimately reject, the basic premises of this philosophy, should pose, and purport to answer, the same riddle.

Descartes's metaphysical revolution, the first important work of reconstruction following the breakdown of medieval scholasticism, was based on a fairly simple principle, a principle that had, however, never previously occurred to anyone. Why not extend the dualism of mind and matter, latent in Western thought since the time of the early Greeks, to its extreme logical conclusion? All matter, including plants, including animals, including corporeal man himself, is nothing but matter and can be understood in terms of the simple mechanical laws of weight and extension. All mind, and this is restricted to God and human reason, is nothing but mind—invisible, intangible, incorporeal and, except when diverted by material influences like the human senses and the human passions, incapable of error.

La Fontaine's sweeping statement, "Everything in the universe speaks," would thus seem to be aimed against another equally sweeping statement: nothing in the universe "speaks" except man because speech—meaningful or expressive behavior of any kind— is an attribute of conscious reason and man alone is endowed with conscious reason.

The same question—Is man, by virtue of his reason, the only animal with the faculty of speech?—had been debated by previous thinkers. Lucretius, in the fifth book of his epic poem *The Nature of Things*, had argued that human speech is not a distinct and separate faculty but an extension of the expressive behavior we observe in animals. Montaigne, in his *Apologie*, had pointed out that animals can, to a certain extent, communicate with men: "They flatter us, threaten us, solicit us, as we do them." That we understand their language no better than we do is as much our fault as theirs.

La Fontaine was acquainted with both these works. In his attacks on Descartes he nonetheless uses Lucretius and Montaigne as predigested by the more orthodox philosopher Gassendi, a contemporary of Descartes and one of his principal antagonists. Fashion as well as prudence pointed in this direction. The major intellectual lion of Madame de La Sablière's salon when La Fontaine first appeared upon the scene was the much-traveled Bernier, a former student and ardent disciple of Gassendi. René Jasinski has shown that La Fontaine's principal attacks on Descartes adhere closely to parallel discussions in Bernier's *Abrégé*, or summary, of Gassendi's philosophy.

La Fontaine, like Gassendi, apparently accepts Descartes's view that man alone is endowed with reflexive reason (IX 20):

Sur tous les animaux enfants du Créateur,
J'ai le don de penser, et je sais que je pense.

Alone of all animals, children of the Creator,
I have the gift of thought, and I know that I think.

But Descartes believed that reflexive reason—the "I know that I know"—is the only form of consciousness. Animals, who do not know that they know, are no more than blind automatons. La Fontaine, following Bernier's *Abrégé* of Gassendi, which, in turn, is following Montaigne's *Apologie*, attempts to undermine Descartes's theory by pointing out that animals have something that is very close to human reason.

This line of attack involves a series of natural science anecdotes, all taken intact from Bernier. The "Discours à Madame de La Sablière" (IX 20) (to be distinguished from the second "Discours" read to the French Academy in 1684) recounts the engineering feats of some presumably Canadian beavers and refers to a tribe of bellicose mammals in Eastern Europe who have carried the art of war to a state of almost human perfection.

The ensuing poem (IX 21) tells how two rats carried an egg back to their home. One lay on his back and clasped the egg with his paws while his companion pulled him along by the tail—a distinctly unpleasant picture. The anecdote of the foresighted owl

(XI 9) is a good deal worse. An owl's nest discovered in an old pine tree was found to contain a large number of plump mice without any feet. The owl, unable to eat them all at the same time, had bitten off their feet to prevent their running away and fattened them up by feeding them grains of wheat.

One would greatly prefer to believe that birds and animals, unlike men and insects, do not engage in this kind of exploitation. La Fontaine, all the eager naturalist, is positively delighted by the thought processes of his repellent owl, which he reconstructs, step by step, like a geometrical theorem. Guaranteeing the authenticity of the anecdote in a footnote, he admits that he may be stretching things a bit in his reconstruction of the owl's thinking. "These exaggerations," La Fontaine maintains, "are permissible in poetry, especially in my particular form of writing." But there is no reason to grant La Fontaine the scientist the poetic license of La Fontaine the fable writer. His anecdote may be true; his interpretation of the anecdote is false, both as science and as poetry.

It is curious to observe how La Fontaine, in his zeal to demonstrate the similarity of animal and human behavior, should so enthusiastically endow his animals with the very traits—calculated industry and violence and avarice—he most deplores in men. As with Montaigne, who also accumulated natural science anecdotes of the kind, the minor premise: animals have something that is very close to human reason, undercuts the major premise: human reason is more of a liability than an asset. And even so, these animals (who seem so much more mechanical than La Fontaine's usual fable characters) offer no conclusive evidence against Descartes's theory of the animal machine.

There is actually no satisfactory way of either proving or disproving Descartes's theory. We can only say that his analogy between natural and mechanical dynamics is unconvincing. This is the line La Fontaine originally takes in the "Discours à

Madame de La Sablière." He first imagines, and very tellingly, how a real animal machine would actually affect us:

> Telle est la montre qui chemine,
> A pas toujours égaux, aveugle et sans dessein.
> Ouvrez-la, lisez dans son sein;
> Mainte roue y tient lieu de tout l'esprit du monde;
> La première y meut la seconde,
> Une troisième suit, elle sonne à la fin.

> Such is the clock that makes its way
> With steps always equal, blind, purposeless.
> Open it, read into its heart;
> Many wheels take the place of all possible mind;
> The first moves the second,
> A third follows, it finally strikes.

As in his mock-heroic account of the Trojan War, the alternation of the two uneven verse lengths conveys a sense of considerable effort: the jerky but deliberate tick-*tock*, tick-*tock* of a run-down clock, a clock that only just manages finally to strike.

La Fontaine then contrasts this animated clockwork monstrosity with a particularly haunting description of an old stag:

>   Cependant quand aux bois
> Le bruit des cors, celui des voix,
> N'a donné nul relâche à la fuyante proie,
> Qu'en vain elle a mis ses efforts
> A confondre et brouiller la voie,
> L'animal chargé d'ans, vieux cerf, et de dix cors,
> En suppose un plus jeune, et l'oblige par force
> A présenter aux chiens une nouvelle amorce.

Yet when in the forest
The sound of horns, that of voices,
Has given no respite to the fleeing prey,
When it has tried in vain
To confuse and blur the track,
The animal burdened with years, an old stag with ten-pronged
antlers,
Starts up a younger one, and forces it
To offer a new bait to the dogs.

The example of the stag at bay is taken from Bernier and La Fontaine, like Bernier, is apparently arguing that the stag's stratagem presupposes something similar to human reason. But La Fontaine is here describing something he had seen for himself and that had apparently struck his imagination. He had already used the example of a stag at bay in the central section of *Psyché* to illustrate his belief, not that animal reasoning is similar to human reasoning but that animal emotions are similar to human emotions. Despite his apparent shift to the Bernier argument, it is the former argument that actually prevails. The whole impact of the passage, as it affects the reader, is emotional, not intellectual: the sheer animal terror of the hunted prey. Could any clock-work mechanism, La Fontaine suggests, affect us as we are affected by a fleeing stag?

It is in this realm of animal, or human, emotions that Descartes's radical divorce of mind and matter becomes most vulnerable. His whole theory of the passions is based on the interaction of the body and the mind. As La Fontaine points out in the conclusion of his "Discours," if mind is totally distinct from matter how can the one act upon the other?

How indeed? The problem has occupied a good many minds before and since. In his "Discours" La Fontaine affirms that the relation of the human body and the human mind is beyond all human comprehension:

L'impression se fait. Le moyen, je l'ignore.
On ne l'apprend qu'au sein de la Divinité;
Et s'il faut en parler avec sincérité,
    Descartes l'ignorait encore.
Nous et lui là-dessus nous sommes tous égaux.

The impression is made. I don't know by what means.
One only learns it in the lap of the gods;
And to speak quite frankly,
    Even Descartes did not know it.
On this point we and he are all equal.

La Fontaine is not criticizing Descartes for his failure to solve
a problem that La Fontaine, like Gassendi, like Montaigne, like
St. Augustine, considered humanly insoluble. He is criticizing
Descartes for his failure to recognize its existence. The anecdote
of the two rats and the egg (IX 21) seems to indicate a possible
approach to the problem, an approach based on Gassendi's interpretation of Lucretius' cosmology
According to this cosmology, as handed down from Democritus to Epicurus and thence to Lucretius, the entire universe, including mind as well as matter, is composed of an infinite number of different atoms which, by combining in different ways,
form all existing phenomena. Gassendi attempted to reconcile
Lucretius' specifically atheist materialism with orthodox Christianity. His theory of the soul, based on a reinterpretation of
Lucretius' distinction between the mind ("animus") and the vital
spirit ("anima"), distinguishes between a material animal soul,
common to men and animals, and an immaterial soul, peculiar
to man. As La Fontaine puts it:

    J'attribuerais à l'animal
Non point une raison selon notre manière,
Mais beaucoup plus aussi qu'un aveugle ressort:

Je subtiliserais un morceau de matière,
Que l'on ne pourrait plus concevoir sans effort,
Quintessence d'atome, extrait de la lumière,
Je ne sais quoi plus vif et plus mobile encor
Que le feu . . .

  I would attribute to the animal
Not our kind of reason,
Yet something much more than a blind mechanism:
I would subtilize a piece of matter,
Until it could be seen only with great difficulty,
Quintessence of atom, extract of light,
Something, as it were, still more rapid and mobile
Than fire . . .

The other soul, common to men and angels,

 Suivrait parmi les airs les célestes phalanges,
 Entrerait dans un point sans en être pressé,
 Ne finirait jamais quoique ayant commencé,
  Choses réelles quoique étranges.

 Would follow the celestial hosts through the air,
 Would be contained in a point without compression,
 Would never end though having begun,
  Things that are real though strange.

It would seem curious that La Fontaine should subscribe so
eagerly to a theory of the soul that brings us right back to the
dualist impasse he points out in the "Discours à Madame de La
Sablière." This underlying conviction that the soul is intimately
connected with the body shows through in his concluding observation that the specifically human soul, which he seems to equate
with conscious reason, is not apparent in small children but

emerges as the child develops physically—a point also emphasized by Lucretius (III 445-450).

La Fontaine's description of the animal and human souls is a good deal vaguer than that of Gassendi. Unlike Gassendi, La Fontaine never explicitly states that the one is completely material, the other completely immaterial. Both seem to imply, in varying degrees, a curious amalgam of material and immaterial qualities. Bernier, for example, describes the animal soul as "a contexture of corpuscles that are very subtle, very mobile or active, similar to those that make fire." La Fontaine, because he is writing as a poet and not as a scientist, avoids this fallacy of misplaced concreteness. His whole description, as he emphasizes by his use of the conditional tense, is based on imaginative analogy, not literal fact. The animal soul might be compared to fire if we could imagine something still more volatile than fire. And to prevent all misunderstanding he adds further images: quintessence of atom, extract of light.

Bernier does not even attempt to describe the human soul, beyond saying that it is immaterial, immortal, intellectual, and angelic. How is it possible to describe something that is completely immaterial? La Fontaine describes the human soul. But, as modern physicists describe the electron or modern psychologists describe the personality, he describes this unknown quantity in terms of its behavior, not its appearance. And the behavior of the human soul is presented as a paradox, or riddle. At one moment it is coursing through the heavens with the celestial hosts; the next moment it is contained in a geometric point. It has originated somewhere; yet it goes on forever.

Both passages (the animal soul "identical in all denizens of the universe that go by the name of animals" and the human soul that "follows the celestial hosts through the air") would seem to refer to Virgil's description of the ancient theory of an ethereal principle that animates all living things and, in its fullest development, creates mind as well as animate life (*Georgics* IV 223-

224 and 226-227). The veiled allusion to the "animus mundi," even though set in two separate contexts, gives a certain continuity to La Fontaine's descriptions of the animal and human souls—an impression supported by the general character of these descriptions.

The whole tenor of La Fontaine's poetry points less to the problem of distinguishing the animal and human souls than to the more basic problem raised in the "Discours à Madame de La Sablière": that of imagining the mysterious conjunction of material and immaterial qualities implied in the phenomenon of animate existence, at any level. La Fontaine's treatment of the fable metaphor suggests the fundamental unity of mind and matter as modes of motion, or energy. Is he not saying more or less the same thing, by way of poetic analogy and poetic paradox, in his description of the animal and human souls?

La Fontaine, unlike Gassendi, may well have recognized this intuition in Lucretius' *Of the Nature of Things.* Lucretius' matter is not the passive substance implied in the Aristotelian, the Cartesian, and, until the recent revolution of nuclear physics, the usual meaning of the word. The "ceaseless motion" (I 999), so fundamental to Lucretius' vision of reality, is built into the structure of his atoms. They are endowed with "mobilitas," the power of movement, which enables them to wander through the great void (II 65).

A similar intuition can be found in certain late-Renaissance thinkers. Leonardo da Vinci conceived reality as a form of energy; Galileo as a form of light. Giordano Bruno, who is believed to have suggested the idea of an infinity of universes to Pascal, asserted, in his *Dialogue on the Infinite,* that all bodies derive their motion from an internal force, not an external motor. La Fontaine's incipient monism is more vaguely suggested. It would have been dangerous, in his day, to be explicit. Bruno had been burned at the stake in 1600. Galileo narrowly escaped a similar fate in

1633. A poet, not a philosopher or a scientist, La Fontaine probably had no desire to be explicit. But he was irresistibly attracted
to the notion of some vital energy, present in all things and the
hidden substratum of all reality—a notion already present in his
descriptions of the fountains of Vaux.

The basin of Neptune, La Fontaine tells us, was created by
a Triton who first petrified a mass of marine monsters

> Avec jus de corail, quintessence de glace,
> Et gorgone dissoute en cristal de Mainsi.

> With coral juice, quintessence of ice,
> And gorgon dissolved in Mainsi crystal.

This magic-by-association, though it produces the reverse effect,
is very similar to that used by La Fontaine in his creation of the
animal soul:

> Je subtiliserais un morceau de matière,
> Que l'on ne pourrait plus concevoir sans effort,
> Quintessence d'atome, extrait de la lumière,
> Je ne sais quoi plus vif et plus mobile encor
> Que le feu . . .

The petrified fountains are then restored to life by the most
powerful of all enchantments operative in La Fontaine's dream
of Vaux: the enchantment of running water.

> Chacun d'eux toutefois conserve sa figure;
> Chacun, sans s'émouvoir, siffle, gronde, murmure,
> Fait que de son fracas tout le mont retentit,
> Et pense avoir encor le gosier trop petit.

On dirait que parfois l'escadron se mutine,
Enivré du nectar d'une source divine;
Il pousse l'onde au ciel, il la darde aux passants,
Semble garder ces lieux en charmes si puissants,
Et défendre l'accès des beautés qu'il nous montre:
L'eau se croise, se joint, s'écarte, se rencontre,
Se rompt, se précipite au travers des rochers,
Et fait comme alambics distiller leurs planchers.

Each one, nonetheless, retains its form;
Each one, though unmoved, whistles, growls, murmurs,
Makes the whole mountain resound with its clangor,
And thinks that its gullet is still too narrow.
At times the squadron seems mutinous,
Intoxicated by some celestial nectar;
It pushes the stream to the sky, shoots it at passers-by,
Seems to guard these places so puissant in charms,
And prohibit our access to the beauties it shows:
The waters cross, join, separate, meet again,
Break off, hurl themselves through some rocks,
And, like alembics, vaporize their floors.

La Fontaine's description of this fountain, pushing its way to
heaven as if intoxicated by some celestial nectar, recalls his description of the human soul following "the celestial hosts through
the air." But the fountain is more exciting. The tenuous imagery
of fire and light, so dear to the metaphysical poets, had less
vitality and power for La Fontaine than the tumultuous and
strident play of spouting water.

La Fontaine would probably have given little thought to the
nature of the human soul had he not become involved in an argument with Descartes. He never tired of gazing at the paradoxical
"liquid crystal," at once fluid and plastic, ethereal and resistant,
always moving, always changing and always building the same

dynamic forms. And he never tired of listening to its hypnotic music. Here was the vital principle of all reality made visible and audible to his delighted eyes and ears!

La Fontaine's later description, in *Psyché*, of the grotto of Thetis at Versailles treats a fountain much as a musical instrument vying, as in a baroque concerto, with the contrasting voices of a nightingale, an echo, and an imaginary flute. (The grotto, destroyed in 1684 to make room for the north wing of the palace, had contained a statue of a young god playing the flute.)

Les oiseaux, envieux d'une telle harmonie,
Epuisent ce qu'ils ont et d'art et de génie;
Philomèle, à son tour, veut s'entendre louer,
Et chante par ressorts que l'onde fait jouer.
Echo même répond, Echo, toujours hôtesse
D'une voûte ou d'un roc témoin de sa tristesse.
L'onde tient sa partie: il se forme un concert
Où Philomèle, l'eau, la flûte, enfin tout sert.

The birds, envying such harmonies,
Show all that they have of both art and genius;
Philomela, in turn, wants her share of the praise,
And sings, borne by the impetus of the stream.
Even Echo answers, Echo, forever a guest
Of a vault or a rock witness to her sadness.
The stream sustains its part: a concert is formed
Where Philomela, water, flute, in fact everything serves.

If a nightingale, an echo, and the statue of a young god playing the flute should be so carried away by the impetus of running water, what of La Fontaine himself who wrote these verses? It is not merely in deference to literary tradition that he sets his muse on the banks of a limpid stream in the "Epilogue" to his eleventh book of fables. La Fontaine's fable poetry is haunted by the sound of running water. But the virtuoso instrument of *Le Songe de Vaux* and *Psyché* here recedes into the background: a faint "basso continuo" behind the dialogue of wolf and lamb, of ant and dove, or the reflections of the solitary heron.

The Language of the Gods

La Fontaine's fables often make fun of the existing conventions of poetry. They are composed of the very elements they ridicule. La Fontaine claims not to have *transcribed* but to have *translated* the voice of nature, as it is expressed by all living things, into the language of the gods, or poetry. Here is the whole art, or artifice, or, as La Fontaine put it, "enchantment" of the fables: La Fontaine's adaptation of the rigid and relatively limited conventions of human discourse to the fugitive and infinitely varied discourse of natural existence.

Valéry made this point in his essay on *Adonis*. "There is a tremendous chasm," he observes, "between the conversation that birds and foliage and ideas hold with us and that which we lend them: an inconceivable gap." The popular image of La Fontaine, the involuntary dreamer, absent-mindedly producing his fables as an apple tree produces apples, must thus be considerably revised. As Valéry says, "It was never a lazy man's game to extract a little grace, a little clarity, a little duration, from the mobility of the things of the mind; and to change that which passes into that which endures. And the more restless and fleeting the desired prey, the greater presence of mind and will power must we have to make it eternally present in its eternally fleeing attitude."

The evanescent reverie that La Fontaine captured and made "eternally present" at the end of the fable of the two pigeons (IX 2) is a good example of the process:

Voilà nos gens rejoints; et je laisse à juger
De combien de plaisirs ils payèrent leurs peines.
Amants, heureux amants, voulez-vous voyager?
    Que ce soit aux rives prochaines;
Soyez-vous l'un à l'autre un monde toujours beau,
    Toujours divers, toujours nouveau;
Tenez-vous lieu de tout, comptez pour rien le reste.
J'ai quelquefois aimé; je n'aurais pas alors
    Contre le Louvre et ses trésors,
Contre le firmament et sa voûte céleste,
    Changé les bois, changé les lieux,
Honorés par les pas, éclairés par les yeux
    De l'aimable et jeune bergère
    Pour qui sous le fils de Cythère
Je servis engagé par mes premiers serments.
Hélas! quand reviendront de semblables moments?
Faut-il que tant d'objets si doux et si charmants
Me laissent vivre au gré de mon âme inquiète?
Ah! si mon cœur osait encor se renflammer!
Ne sentirai-je plus de charme qui m'arrête?
    Ai-je passé le temps d'aimer?

Our friends are now reunited; you may judge for yourself
With how many pleasures they paid for their pains.
Lovers, happy lovers, do you want to travel?
    Let it be to the nearest shores;
Be, one for the other, an always beautiful world,
    Always varied, always new;
Be everything for yourselves, forget all the rest.
Once I was in love; I would not then,
    Not for the Louvre and its treasures,
Not for the firmament and its celestial vault,
    Have changed the woods, changed the places,
Honored by the steps, lit by the eyes
    Of the gracious young shepherdess
    For whom under Cythera's son
I served bound by my first vows.
Alas! when will moments like these return?
Must so many objects, so tender, so charming,
Let me live at the pleasure of my restless soul?
Ah! if only my heart dared catch fire again!
Will no charm ever arrest me again?
    Am I too old for love?

"Who among us," Baudelaire once asked, "has not, in his ambitious moments, dreamed of a poetic prose, musical without rhythm and without rhyme, sufficiently supple and sufficiently abrupt to adapt itself to the movements of the soul, to the rise and fall of reverie, to the sudden shocks of consciousness?" In one sense this is a remarkably accurate description of La Fontaine's poem: a gradual expansion of delighted reverie sinks back into actuality, then vanishes with the "sudden shock of consciousness," am I too old for love? But, contrary to Baudelaire's dream of a "poetic prose" devoid of rhyme and rhythm, La Fontaine, exploiting the existing instruments of French poetry, has given these inconsistent "movements of the soul" the concrete shape and imperious necessity of a recognizable aesthetic form.

La Fontaine's over-all theme, an antithesis between the space world of travelers and the private world of lovers, is somewhat similar to that of Donne's "The Canonization." Unlike Donne, however, La Fontaine presents the theme not as a triumphant assertion about love but as an ideal for other lovers or an idealized reminiscence. And he develops the antithesis not as the intellectual structure but as the unconscious, and partly hidden, substratum of his poem, a poem that progresses not as a logical development but by way of rhyme and rhythm and the loose association of ideas. The passage may be divided into four segments, each characterized by a sudden change of tone and of perspective: (1) verses 1 and 2, which conclude the fable anecdote; (2) verses 3-7, an apostrophe to lovers in general; (3) verses 8-15, the poet's idealized reminiscence; (4) verses 16-21, his consideration of his present situation.

Each segment constitutes, in a varying degree, a digression from the previous segment. The most striking of these is the sudden switch from the theme of friendship, on which the fable is actually based, to that of love. But there are no logical transitions in the ensuing switches from the general to the particular, from reminiscence to actuality. La Fontaine is apparently imitating the irrational digressions of consciousness. The transitions are facilitated by La Fontaine's irregular verse form, which allows him to glide, almost imperceptibly, from one level of poetry to another. And the passage is tied to the fable, and unified itself, by the underlying antithesis between the superficial outer world of emotional dispersion and the rich inner world of emotional concentration.

Another important unifying factor is the rhyme scheme which, until the very last verse, never quite coincides with the sense units. One could diagram this as follows:

```
                 a b a b c c d e e d  f  f  g  g  h  h  h  i  j  i  j
rhyme scheme       1         2          3              4

verses           1 2 3 4 5 6 7 8 9 10 11 12 13 14 15 16 17 18 19 20 21

sense units        1       2              3                4
                 fable apostrophe     idealized        return to
                 end   to lovers      reminiscence     actuality
```

Each new idea or change of tone thus springs from the previous idea or tone with a powerful internal necessity, not the necessity of logic but that of rhyme. One could approximate the structure with a poem written in separate stanzas in which the sentences always begin and end in the middle of a stanza. The effect would seem more conscious, however, and consequently less justifiable.

Voilà nos gens rejoints; et je laisse à juger
De combien de plaisirs ils payèrent leurs peines.
Amants, heureux amants, voulez-vous voyager?
    Que ce soit aux rives prochaines;
Soyez-vous l'un à l'autre un monde toujours beau,
    Toujours divers, toujours nouveau;
Tenez-vous lieu de tout, comptez pour rien le reste.

The first two verses, which conclude the fable anecdote, are
not very rhythmic alexandrins. The enjambment destroys the
pause at the end of the first verse and the caesura in the second
verse is fairly weak. The sense of diminishing intensity, characteristic of La Fontaine's concluding verses, conveys the impression: this is the end of the poem. The effect is supported by
the reiterated *b* and *p* sounds in the second alexandrin: the final
flourish of some tuneless percussion instrument.

At the same time the rhyme scheme informs us that this is
a false ending. The two initial alexandrins are a tiny recitative
leading up to the aria, which La Fontaine attacks with the
strongly accented "Amants, heureux amants"—a characteristic La
Fontaine aria opening (IV 1):

> Amour, amour, quand tu nous tiens . . .
>
> Love, love, when you possess us . . .

in *Psyché*:

> Volupté, Volupté, qui fus jadis maîtresse . . .
>
> Volupté, Volupté, erstwhile mistress . . .

and in another fable (VII 12):

> Le repos, le repos, trésor si précieux . . .
>
> Tranquillity, tranquillity, so precious a treasure . . .

The beat is sustained by the parallel "voulez-vous," "soyez-
vous," "tenez-vous" constructions and the reiterated "toujours."
A melody emerges, built around La Fontaine's soft, enticing *v*,
ge, *che*, and *j* sounds in combination with frequent *r*'s.

J'ai quelquefois aimé; je n'aurais pas alors
    Contre le Louvre et ses trésors,
Contre le firmament et sa voûte céleste,
    Changé les bois, changé les lieux,
Honorés par les pas, éclairés par les yeux . . .

The melody now drops into a lower key. The subject, lovers, shifts to the first person singular; the imperative tense to the past, and then the conditional tense; the crucial verb "aimé" is used for the first time, in naked simplicity, without an object. At the same time the beat quickens, a powerful pulsating beat conveyed by parallel or antithetical constructions within the alternating alexandrins and octosyllables.

    De l'aimable et jeune bergère
    Pour qui sous le fils de Cythère
Je servis engagé par mes premiers serments.

The movement now swells into a long, sustained period of two octosyllables and an alexandrin completely devoid of punctuation. (One would at least expect "sous le fils de Cythère" to be set off by commas and one would expect another comma after "Je servis.") This breathless sweep is the climax of the whole passage. We must now stop for a new breath, and the breath, very naturally, takes the form of a sigh, "Hélas!" bringing us back to emotional as well as respiratory realities.

Hélas! quand reviendront de semblables moments?
Faut-il que tant d'objets si doux et si charmants
Me laissent vivre au gré de mon âme inquiète?
Ah! si mon cœur osait encor se renflammer!
Ne sentirai-je plus de charme qui m'arrête?
    Ai-je passé le temps d'aimer?

The passage draws to a close with five melodious but sober alexandrins, La Fontaine's "middle voice." They are as beautiful as the quasi-Romantic alexandrins of Venus's lament for Adonis; and they are entirely different. La Fontaine is not imitating the passionate cry of the human voice, inevitably a bit theatrical. He is letting us overhear a contained, a controlled, a barely whispered internal drama. One cannot read these verses in the intense, sustained legato of Venus's lament. Masculine syllable endings predominate. Each sentence, either a question or an exclamation, is enclosed in a little zone of silence which interrupts the accumulated momentum of the alexandrins, of the emotion itself. The melody moves more and more slowly, bringing us to the crucial question:

Ne sen*ti*rai-*je* plus de *c*harme qui m'ar*rê*te?

This haunting, fluent alexandrin, structured around the *t-r-j ch-r-t* pattern, contains a hidden sting: the sharp bite of the initial and terminal *t*'s, cutting into the soft, hypnotic "charme," or enchantment, of remembered delights.

The final octosyllable—"Ai-je passé le temps d'aimer?"—is, in view of the six preceding alexandrins, virtually floating in space. Not only does this verse, instinctively drawn out to compensate for the four missing syllables, move extremely slowly; it actually incorporates a few seconds of the general silence following the conclusion of the poem—a subtle but nonetheless discernible effect which in musical notation would be conveyed by a rest. The passage, rather than ending on a note of positive finality, fades into the vast potentialities of silence. The effect, which depends on our recognition of the inconclusive octosyllable as the conclusion of the poem, has been prepared by the construction of the passage as a whole. Here at long last the sense units and rhyme schemes, which have been evading each other for twenty verses, exactly coincide.

The conclusion of the fable of the two pigeons is a particularly good example of La Fontaine's poetic technique as it is possible to identify some of the raw material that went into it. The idea expressed in the appeal to happy lovers is less simple than it seems. As Arthur Lovejoy has pointed out, there is a definite argument, inherited from Plato's *Timaeus* and current among seventeenth-century theologists, that the divine origin of the world is reflected in its diversity as well as in its perfection: "it is in the consideration of the diversity of existent things that we come . . . to realize the infinite variety which . . . is of the essence of the Divine Reason."

La Fontaine alluded directly to this argument in a letter to Saint-Evremond (1687):

> Rien ne m'engage à faire un livre;
> Mais la raison m'oblige à vivre
> En sage citoyen de ce vaste Univers;
> Citoyen qui, voyant un monde si *divers,*
> Rend à son auteur les hommages
> Que méritent de tels ouvrages.

> Nothing forces me to write a book;
> But reason compels me to live
> As a good citizen of this vast Universe;
> Citizen who, seeing so varied a world,
> Renders its author the homage
> That such works deserve.

Donne's lovers' world is a concentrated reflection of the existing world. La Fontaine's "un monde toujours beau, toujours *divers,* toujours nouveau" arrogates the "Divine Reason" of God the creator to happy lovers.

His reminiscence of an early love affair borrows a figure previously used in a different poem. A verse passage contained in a letter to the elegant Duchesse de Bouillon, written (1671) several years before the fable of the two pigeons was published, opens as follows:

> Peut-on s'ennuyer en des lieux
> Honorés par les pas, éclairés par les yeux
>   D'une aimable et vive princesse . . .

> How can one be bored in a place
> Honored by the steps, lit by the eyes
>   Of a gracious and spritely princess . . .

The alexandrin which La Fontaine transcribed in his fable is an ingenious way of imagining a lovely woman's influence on her environment. In the letter it seems casual, inconsequential, a bit offhand. The tone is that of a gallant man of the world paying his respects to a reigning beauty. This is partly because the verse is written in the present tense; it is hard to take poetic figures like the one La Fontaine uses seriously unless they are colored by the magic of remembrance. And it is partly because the verse is not supported by its context. In the fable, where it acquires considerable intensity, the figure is presented as a reminiscence and is supported by the over-all antithesis of the space macrocosm and the love microcosm. The meter also fits into a pattern established by the preceding verses: the uneven and highly emotional pulse of alternating alexandrins and octosyllables.

"D'une aimable et vive princesse" is again a fairly casual statement as compared to the tender "De l'aimable et jeune bergère" of the fable. A young shepherdess suggests a softer emotion than a spritely princess and La Fontaine has changed the indefinite "a" into an irreplaceable "the." The new epithet also permits La Fontaine to use softer consonant and vowel sounds and to establish one of his characteristic sound patterns—*l-b-l j-b-g*—that gives the verse an incantatory quality.

About halfway through the poem addressed to the Duchesse de Bouillon is a verse somewhat similar to the final octosyllable of the fable: "Pour moi, le temps d'aimer est passé, je l'avoue" ("For me, the time for love has passed, I admit"). The characteristic La Fontaine touch in this Horatian sentiment is "le temps d'aimer"—an expression that implies a parallel between the seasonal mating periods of animals and the longer, but non-recurrent, season of human love. One is reminded of the last-minute love affair of his procrastinating lark (IV 22). In the improvised verses La Fontaine seems to have written this down as it occurred to him without giving much thought to problems of composition. In the fable he hit on the idea of playing up the transitional, offhand phrase by putting it at the rhyme and using it as the conclusion to his entire poem. Instead of giving it an air of finality, which would have sounded a bit self-important, he deliberately emphasizes its lack of finality by turning the positive statement into a question, the alexandrin into an octosyllable.

Another recognizable piece of raw material that La Fontaine has worked into the conclusion of his fable is the lover's rejection of various worldly domains in favor of his mistress. Like Laforgue, who sometimes paraphrased French folk songs in his poetry, and Eliot, who fitted "Here we go round the mulberry bush" into "The Hollow Men," La Fontaine is imitating a traditional theme in old French folk songs like "Auprès de ma blonde" or "Si le roi m'avait donné Paris sa grand' ville"—the song sung by Molière's Misanthrope as an antidote to the sonnet of the literary Marquis.

The theme, like the verses transposed from the letter to the Duchesse de Bouillon, corresponds to the over-all theme of La Fontaine's fable. It is particularly appropriate for the aria segment of the fable. For La Fontaine, as for the Misanthrope, it no doubt spelled simplicity, spontaneity, sincerity, all the qualities so noticeably lacking in contemporary salon poetry. There is nothing simple about La Fontaine's elaboration of the theme. The Louvre and its treasures, an octosyllable, is echoed in the parallel but expanded figure of the firmament and its celestial vault, an alexandrin. The traditional folk song expresses a preference for one's mistress as opposed to various worldly domains. La Fontaine goes this one better by preferring the restricted localities that have merely been frequented by his mistress to the celestial vault itself—a figure leading up to the highly literary reference to Cythera's son (i.e., Cupid). This unexpectedly sophisticated treatment of a simple theme gives the passage its special charm. The folk song justifies what might otherwise seem the empty hyperboles of La Fontaine's gallantry; the gallantry keeps us from taking the folk song too seriously.

Suppose La Fontaine had imitated the simplicity of the folk song: would he not then have seemed a little too "sincere" and, consequently, bordered on "insincerity"? Forestalling the possible skepticism of the reader, La Fontaine deliberately heightens the figures of the folk song, soaring higher and higher until he eventually finds himself speaking in the breathless circumlocutions of a literary marquis, and it is high time to return to earth. All right, La Fontaine implies, perhaps I *am* exaggerating a little bit; but let me enjoy my memories; they are about all I have left. The counterpoetry, thus limiting the poetry, gives it a keener edge—not the sardonic humor of Laforgue's and Eliot's modernized folk songs but that conjunction of lyric emotion and ironic awareness we find in Horace, in Marvell, or in La Fontaine's fable of the uprooted oak. It is a way of telling us that poetry, whether in poetry or in life, is a momentary illumination. When, like La Fontaine's wolf, we try to seize hold of the "orbicular image" of the moon-cheese it disappears.

The message is actually implied in the over-all structure of the passage. This is the structure of the daydream at the end of the fable of the milkmaid (VII 10): after soaring to precarious pinnacles of fame and glory La Fontaine founders on some accidental shock of consciousness and "Je suis Gros-Jean comme devant" ("I am just plain Jean again"). It is the structure of the soliloquy at the end of the fable of the Mogul's dream (XI 4): after opening with the "Oh, how I love Solitude!" characteristic of early seventeenth-century lyric poetry, La Fontaine abandons the rhapsodic "I" of Saint-Amant and Théophile for the sober, reflective "I" of Virgil's humble prayer to the Muses (*Georgics* II 475-489). It is the structure of the fable of the fox and the crow. It is the structure of the fable form itself: the effervescent poetry of lyric emotion rises and falls within the resistant counterpoetry of objective fact—a trajectory to some extent visible upon the printed page.

V

A Citizen of the Universe

A Citizen of the Universe

La Fontaine took considerable satisfaction in the fact that his fables were an entirely original poetic genre. He took equal satisfaction in the fact that the later fables, Books VII through XII, fit into a certain tradition of poetry: the great Latin tradition of the first century B.C.

La Fontaine, by this time an old man, expressed his debt to classical antiquity in the *Epître* to the Bishop of Soissons (1687), his contribution to the Battle of the Ancients and the Moderns. His tone, which is moderate and circumspect, indicates a polite refusal to become deeply involved in this most passionate and irrelevant of literary issues. His verdict is nonetheless clear and, negatively, exactly similar to that of Apollo in his early comedy *Clymène*: contemporary poetry in France has reached a dead end. Malherbe and Racan were the last great poets and they took their lyres with them when they died. Unlike the Apollo of *Clymène* who, though recommending Horace as a model, seems skeptical of the possibility of successful imitation, La Fontaine now claims that he has discovered a good way out of the impasse: a return to the great highway of classical antiquity. "We get lost," he asserts, "when we try other paths."

The argument, as presented by La Fontaine, raises the more general question: how far is it legitimate for a poet to imitate other poets? La Fontaine's answer is typically pragmatic. Anything that works is permissible in poetry. Thus, while there is no sense in imitation for the sake of imitation, neither is there any sense in originality for the sake of originality.

La Fontaine claims that he "merely" appropriates the ideas, the style, and the rules of classical poetry, not to mention any incidental passages that happen to strike his fancy. And he is not exaggerating. In his later fables La Fontaine paraphrases innumerable passages of Latin poetry. But—and this is the real test —the transported passages blend as easily and naturally into the context of the fables as do the proverbs and the folk sayings. La Fontaine has assimilated not merely the conventions and figures of Latin poetry but the vital spirit that lies behind them: the Latin view of nature not as a décor or a source of analogies for human events and situations but as a general ordering of all reality, this reality including man.

The eighteenth-century philosopher was proud to consider himself a citizen of the world. La Fontaine, faithful to the spirit of Lucretius, chose a less parochial title. I must try to live, he wrote his friend Saint-Evremond (1687), "En sage citoyen de ce vaste Univers"—as a good citizen of this vast Universe.

The Latin view of nature, as set forth in Lucretius' *Of the Nature of Things*, establishes a very distant, very long-range view of man—a perspective similar to that of the Oriental fables La Fontaine uses in addition to Aesopian and other sources in Books VII-XII. The human animal, generally the focal point of his own preoccupations, becomes no more than an incidental part of a transcendent whole, a whole which, according to Lucretius, includes an infinity of universes. Seen from this angle, he inevitably assumes a poignantly comic, or tragic, absurdity—like a character in a play who remains ignorant of an essential truth that has been revealed to the audience. How futile, how senseless, our ordinary human preoccupations! What a painful, pointless struggle after the will-o'-the-wisps of prestige, power, fame, and glory in an impossible effort to transcend or, as Pascal believed, at least forget the natural limitations imposed on all living things! We are beaten before we even start.

Lucretius believed he could teach men to rise above their dismal fate. "Don't be an actor in so trivial and brief a farce," he pleads. Be, in spirit if not in fact, a member of the audience. Renounce all the pleasures and pains, all the hopes and fears, of normal human existence and be content to see things as they really are. "The dread and darkness of the mind" will then be dispelled and we will be able to consider our fate with the calm indifference of an outside observer.

La Fontaine's fable of Death and the dying man (VIII 1), is imitated from a famous passage in *Of the Nature of Things* where Lucretius imagines what Nature would say to an old man who is reluctant to die (III 931-1052). In La Fontaine's fable it is Death, not Nature, who does the talking, but she uses the same arguments, often the same words: There is no use delaying any longer; you have had your life and must make room for others who will take your place. Yet La Fontaine, though theoretically in agreement with Lucretius' arguments, does not seem to find them very helpful. It would indeed be admirable, he observes, if old people departed this life considerately and promptly as a guest departs from a banquet. It would also be pointless, as well as tactless, to go and shout this to a dying man.

> J'ai beau te le crier; mon zèle est indiscret:
> Le plus semblable aux morts meurt le plus à regret.

> It's no use shouting at you; my zeal is indiscreet:
> He who is most like the dead dies most reluctantly.

One detects a lurking sympathy for Lucretius' despised "cupiditas vitae," that vital impulse for continued survival, no matter what the terms, that La Fontaine described so eloquently in the earlier fable of Death and the woodsman (I 16).

La Fontaine may have admired the Lucretian ideal; he apparently considered it unattainable among humanity at large. What passes for Epicurean philosophy in La Fontaine's fables is actually Horace's greatly mitigated version of the doctrine. Once having accepted this existence on its own terms as brief, uncertain, and final, let us artificially re-create, each man for himself, the outward conditions of the Golden Age. Let us avoid all hazardous adventures, abandon the pointless struggle for fame and wealth and power, and quietly enjoy the good things of life during the brief time allotted us (a course made possible by cutting down on unnecessary luxuries but which nonetheless supposes a certain minimum of economic security; a private income or a generous Maecenas is a necessary attribute of the Horatian code). As for the rest, let us try to accept our fate with grace and humor.

Whenever La Fontaine develops any of these themes he is apt to quote or paraphrase Horace. What is particularly Horatian in La Fontaine's later fables is a sort of humorous resignation to the irrationality and complexity of human existence, La Fontaine himself included. It is really more a question of tone than of theme: the dead-pan humor and contained emotion expressed in sudden, yet apparently natural, shifts of mood or of perspective; the swift transitions from the general to the particular, from lofty theories to humble facts, from a mood of lyric abandon or moral righteousness to one of half-mocking self-awareness. The characteristic themes themselves, like so many other themes La Fontaine uses, seem to be pretexts rather than deeply assimilated truths. Horace's modus vivendi was a bit too pale, too gentlemanly, for La Fontaine's restless mind and ardent sensibility.

La Fontaine seems to have been attracted by the gentle, reflective version of Lucretius that he found in Virgil's *Georgics*: the prayer to the Muses (II 475-489) that he paraphrases (XI 4); the description of the poor but contented gardener (IV 125-148) to which he refers (XII 20). But the fundamental morality of the *Georgics* is not one of contemplation but one of action. The moral of the poem, spelled out again and again as Virgil describes the farmer's unremitting round of tasks, is the importance and dignity of labor, both as a means to a practical end and as a necessary human discipline.

The *Georgics* play an important role in La Fontaine's later fables, but most decidedly not the moral of the *Georgics*. Labor, of any kind, was not an activity La Fontaine particularly admired. When he goes so far as to idealize the natural life he celebrates the gardener, enclosed in his tiny oasis of fruits and flowers, not the rough plowman.

No one of the available moral life lines—Lucretius' philosophy of detachment, Horace's philosophy of moderation, Virgil's philosophy of work—proved satisfactory for La Fontaine. Would any moral philosophy have satisfied him? There is something a bit discouraging in any systematic analysis of the human situation to the extent that it puts us in the role of a detached observer. How dull and pointless life can seem when we are watching it from the outside! How beautiful and exciting when we are engaged in the actual process of living! It was La Fontaine's disruptive cheerfulness, his wholehearted enjoyment of the passing moment that, balancing his bitter view of human destiny, seems to have interfered with his vocation as a philosopher. As he so joyously proclaims at the end of *Psyché*, in what seems a complete travesty of Epicurean ethics:

Volupté, Volupté, qui fus jadis maîtresse
    Du plus bel esprit de la Grèce,
Ne me dédaigne pas, viens-t'en loger chez moi;
    Tu n'y seras pas sans emploi.
J'aime le jeu, l'amour, les livres, la musique,
La ville et la campagne, enfin tout; il n'est rien
    Qui ne me soit souverain bien,
Jusqu'au sombre plaisir d'un cœur mélancolique.

Volupté,* Volupté, erstwhile mistress
  Of the prettiest wit in Greece,
Disdain me not, come live with me;
  You will be well occupied.
I love cards and love and books and music,
The city, the country, in fact everything; there is nothing
  That is not my greatest good,
Even the somber pleasure of a melancholy heart.

In the second "Discours à Madame de La Sablière," which he read to the French Academy in 1684, La Fontaine, now in his sixties, abandons all further efforts to follow the precepts of the wise philosopher, whether Epicurean, Stoic, or Christian. Madame de La Sablière, recently converted to Christianity, had apparently been attempting to persuade La Fontaine to lead a more orderly existence. La Fontaine agrees that his life is disorderly in the extreme. He has wasted his best years on

  Les pensers amusants, les vagues entretiens,
  Vains enfants du loisir, délices chimériques,
  Les romans, et le jeu, peste des républiques . . .

  Diverting ideas, aimless conversations,
  Futile children of leisure, chimerical delights,
  Novels, and cards, the bane of republics . . .

Worse still, he now has little time left for improvement. But it is no use:

  Ne point errer est chose au-dessus de mes forces . . .

  To quit my errant ways is beyond my powers . . .

* This word, since it conveys a conjunction of sensual and spiritual delight, has no Anglo-Saxon equivalent.

Here is the same La Fontaine who sixteen years earlier, in his hymn to Volupté, declared his indiscriminate love of cards, love, books, music, the city, the country—everything. He now realizes how far he departs from the precepts of Epicurus. The tone is no longer one of self-approbation but of apparent self-deprecation. Had La Fontaine been truly ashamed of his unepicurean diversions, would he have made them sound so eminently delightful? While appearing to strike an appropriate attitude of shame and remorse, La Fontaine is actually suggesting that Epicurean "peace of mind" precludes the most desirable pleasures of human existence.

In one of his last fables (XII 20), first published in 1685, La Fontaine openly condemns the negativistic morality of retrenchment. He is actually referring to the Stoics, but his criticism applies equally well to the Epicureans:

Ils font cesser de vivre avant que l'on soit mort.

They make you stop living before you are dead.

In "The daughters of Minos," also published in 1685, La Fontaine again observes: why should we aspire to a state of mind that is little more than a living death?

Les morts sont donc heureux? Ce n'est pas mon avis . . .

So the dead are happy? This is not my opinion . . .

The "Discours à Madame de La Sablière" carries a further and more important implication. Poetry was "the bane" of at least one austere Republic. It is La Fontaine's very inability to achieve the sublime detachment of the philosopher, his very immersion in the flux of terrestrial existence, that marks him as a poet— not in the restricted sense of Malherbe or Boileau but in the full sense that Plato has given to the word:

Je m'avoue, il est vrai, s'il faut parler ainsi,
Papillon de Parnasse, et semblable aux abeilles
A qui le bon Platon compare nos merveilles.
Je suis chose légère, et vole à tout sujet . . .

I confess myself, it is true, to speak in these terms,
A Parnassus butterfly, and like the bees
To which the excellent Plato compares our marvels.
I am a light thing, and fly to all subjects . . .

La Fontaine the poet, curiously enough, has a good deal in common with Lucretius the poet. It is true that La Fontaine's hymn to Volupté reveals a complete misunderstanding of the ethics of Epicurus, who must have turned in his grave when he heard himself referred to as "the prettiest wit in Greece." "Voluptas," as propounded by Lucretius the Epicurean moralist, is a state of inner tranquillity obtained by abdicating all personal hopes and fears; it is a way of avoiding pain, and pleasure too in so far as pleasure is a potential source of pain (III 28). But La Fontaine's error should actually be ascribed to Lucretius.

The hymn to Volupté is imitated from Lucretius' opening invocation to Venus, source of all animate life and delight ("voluptas") of men and gods. This highly unorthodox use of the key word of Epicurean ethics betrays an inner contradiction in Lucretius' poem: his dual conception of nature as an existing fact, which he surveys with the calm indifference of an outside observer, and as a mysterious, compelling force, which he experiences, as in his opening invocation, with something approaching religious awe. Lucretius the Epicurean moralist invites us to detach ourselves from the endless circuit of natural existence and attain within ourselves the impassivity of the gods. Lucretius the poet hurls us back in as eager children of life-giving Venus through whom "all things are conceived and come forth to look at the light of the sun" (I 5).

A similar contradiction appears in Virgil's *Georgics*. While Virgil the agricultural expert is describing the arduous, unremitting labors of the farmer, Virgil the poet, who owes much to Lucretius the poet, is celebrating the passionate, involuntary joys and sorrows of growing plants and animals. It was a Victorian moralist who, so unperceptively, hit on the bee as a symbol of industry. Virgil's bees, in striking antithesis to the explicit moral of his poem, are ecstatic voluptuaries and gallant warriors.

Here is the same conjunction of counterpoetry and poetry that we find in La Fontaine's fables. I am not particularly interested in writing poetry, the poet warns us, for poetry is no more than an agreeable fiction, and I intend to tell the truth. Lucretius asserts that he has merely coated his bitter and otherwise unpalatable theme with "the sweet honey of the Muses." His object is to reveal the true "nature of things" (I 945-950). Virgil assures his patron, Maecenas: "I will not waste your time with poetic fictions and digressions and long-winded rhetoric" but deal directly and concisely with the essential facts (*Georgics* II 45-46). La Fontaine, in the preface to his first volume of fables, observes: "The value of this work should not be judged in terms of its form so much as its utility." Truth, the considered judgment of a detached observer, limits the "poetry," the imaginative vision of an enthusiastic participant. But the flame of poetry burns all the more brightly against the sober background of Lucretius' cosmology, Virgil's agricultural precepts, and La Fontaine's fable common sense. At a certain level of intensity it becomes a form of truth—no less real and no less universal than the truth of the detached observer.

Virgil's treatment of his plants, birds, animals, and insects departs fairly widely from his professed intention to adhere strictly to sober, agricultural fact. But it corresponds to his actual vision of reality.

Take, for example, Virgil's battle of the bees (*Georgics* IV 67-86). How are we to interpret this famous passage? The whole description is based on the analogy of human warfare and is written in traditional epic style, a style very similar to that of the *Aeneid*. Is Virgil perfectly serious about his bees or is he engaging in a form of mock-heroic poetry? Neither of the alternative interpretations is really possible. Virgil's whole attitude toward his bees is serious and his description is intended to be realistic. Yet he must certainly have realized that it involves a somewhat unexpected juxtaposition of two antithetical scales: Homeric and apian combat. There is an element of humor in the passage, but not the usual humor of mock-heroic poetry. Virgil wants to surprise or disconcert his reader. But, like Jupiter's monkey, his reason for doing so is to invalidate our normal hierarchization of reality. Bees as well as warriors will lay down their lives for their queen (Virgil thought it was a king) and this similarity is more important than the difference in scale. His later comparison of the bees building their honeycombs to Cyclops forging giant bolts carries the same point a little further.

Montaigne observed that, as seen by God, the outcome of a battle is no more important than the hop of a flea. Here is the central theme of Virgil's poem: I work in little things but, for the poet, they have their glory ("gloria") too: the glory of all natural things from the upheaval of the ocean to the trembling of a leaf; not the charm of a miniature or a vignette.

A situation similar to Virgil's battle of the bees arises in the first fable of La Fontaine's second volume of fables, the animals stricken by the plague (VII 1):

Ils ne mouraient pas tous, mais tous étaient frappés.
   On n'en voyait point d'occupés
A chercher le soutien d'une mourante vie;
   Nul mets n'excitait leur envie.
   Ni loups ni renards n'épiaient
   La douce et l'innocente proie.
   Les tourterelles se fuyaient;
   Plus d'amour, partant plus de joie.

All did not die, but all were stricken.
　　One saw none engaged
In seeking subsistence for a dying life;
　　No food excited their appetite.
　　Neither wolves nor foxes were on the watch
　　For the gentle and innocent prey.
　　The turtledoves avoided each other;
　　No more love, and so no more joy.

If we approach this passage from the perspective established by the first six books of fables we are very likely to detect a note of literary parody, a parody of either Thucydides's or Lucretius' description of the Athens plague. But parody of this kind has little point unless it contains some element of incongruity and there is no real incongruity in La Fontaine's description. Animals as well as human beings can be stricken by a plague.

The passage is taken, and it is taken straight, from Virgil's description of an animal plague that once broke out in a northern province (*Georgics* III 478-566). Two verses directly paraphrase Virgil's: "Nor did the treacherous wolf prowl around the sheep" (537). Virgil, when he wrote this description, was thinking of Lucretius, but he never intended it as a parody of Lucretius; it is the common denominator, not the discrepancies, of human and animal existence that stands uppermost in his mind.

The problem again arises in La Fontaine's description of a vanquished cock (VII 13):

Il alla se cacher au fond de sa retraite,
　　Pleura sa gloire et ses amours,
Ses amours, qu'un rival tout fier de sa défaite
Possédait à ses yeux. Il voyait tous les jours
Cet objet rallumer sa haine et son courage.
Il aiguisait son bec, battait l'air et ses flancs,
　　Et, s'exerçant contre les vents,
　　S'armait d'une jalouse rage.

He went and hid at the far end of his shelter,
    Lamented his glory and his loves,
His loves, which a rival gloating over his defeat
Enjoyed in his presence. Every day he saw
This object rekindle his hate and his courage.
He sharpened his beak, beat the air and his wings,
    And, practicing against the winds,
    Armed himself with a jealous rage.

This passage, particularly in view of La Fontaine's previous reference to the Trojan War, perhaps implies an ironic reference to Achilles' angry withdrawal to his tent. Yet cocks, as well as men, are subject to love and defeat and humiliation. There is an element of humor but not of incongruity in La Fontaine's description. It is imitated from Virgil's description of a defeated bull (*Georgics* III 224-236).

Traditional fable symbolism, with its careful separation of virtues and vices, is rudely shaken by the passages La Fontaine imitated from Virgil's *Georgics*. We can see this in his rather unexpected association of rapacious carnivores and amorous turtle-doves as parallel instances of weakened vitality in the fable of the animals stricken by the plague. The passage is very Lucretian in spirit: a healthy world must make room for Mars as well as Venus.

We see it again in La Fontaine's description of the spider's enemy, the swallow, catching flies on the wing (X 6):

La sœur de Philomèle, attentive à sa proie,
Malgré le bestion happait mouches dans l'air,
Pour ses petits, pour elle, impitoyable joie . . .

Philomela's sister, attentive to her prey,
Despite the beastule snapped flies in the air,
For her young, for herself, pitiless joy . . .

The epithet "pitiless," as applied to a carefree swallow, is somewhat surprising. It is taken from Virgil's description of swallows and other insect-eating birds catching bees on the wing as food for their "pitiless nestlings" (IV 16-17).

La Fontaine's earlier description of the swallow, "Caracolant, frisant l'air et les eaux"—caracoling, skimming the air and the waters—is reminiscent of a bird in the *Aeneid* (IV 253-257). There is a typically Virgilian grandeur in the all-inclusive denomination of sea and sky and a typically Virgilian disruption of our normal human sense of scale in the evocation of the tiny swallow joyfully skirting the edges of their vast domains.

This disruption of our normal human sense of scale is not simply a literary device; like Lucretius' invocation to Venus, it expresses the underlying unity of all animate existence—the plants, the insects, the animals—all dignified, and in a sense equalized, by their common participation in the workings of the natural universe.

Horace, the urban poet, often emphasizes the irrelevance of human differences of wealth and station in view of the universal eventuality of death, a theme that has been used and reused a good many times since Horace. Virgil emphasizes the irrelevance of different forms of life in view of the universal fact of life itself. Two passages most strikingly convey the theme. One is Virgil's description of the passion of love: "All earthly species, both men and wild animals, the ocean people, flocks and brightly colored birds hurl themselves into the frenzy and the fire: love is the same for all." (*Georgics* III 242-244). The other is his description of the ethereal spirit that animates all earthly things: "From this flocks, herds, men, all kinds of wild animals, and whatever is born derive their subtle spirits" (IV 223-224).

Both passages, significantly, were paraphrased by La Fontaine. The first in a description of spring, the season of love (IV 22):

                                        . . . le temps
Que tout aime, et que tout pullule dans le monde:

Monstres marins au fond de l'onde,
Tigres dans les forêts, alouettes aux champs.

. . . the time
When everything falls in love and everything multiplies:
Sea monsters in the depths of the waves,
Tigers in the forests, larks in the fields.

The second in his description of the animal soul, identical in all "denizens of the universe that go by the name of animals" (IX 21).

Nature for Lucretius and Virgil and La Fontaine is, on the one hand, the irreducible counterpoetry of Epicurean cosmology and agriculture and deflationary fable common sense. It is also the poetry of animate existence: an existence governed in part by Mars, the agent of violence and death and destruction, yet constantly renewed and sanctified by Venus, the goddess of love and procreation and the mysterious, inexplicable joy of simply being alive and able "to look at the light of the sun."

Lucretius' introductory invocation to Venus is a particularly powerful example of this poetry, an example Virgil often had in mind when he was writing his *Georgics*. How joyfully Virgil's bees welcome the new summer! "When the golden sun has driven winter underground and opens the sky with summer light, they forthwith wander through the glades and forests and harvest the brilliant flowers and lightly sip the surfaces of streams. Then, glad with some unfathomable joy ("nescio qua dulcedine"), they tend their grubs and cells . . ." (IV 51-56).

How eagerly his crows chatter together after a thunderstorm has cleared! "Then the crows sigh gently, three or four low calls, and often, in their high chambers, especially gladdened by some unfathomable joy, chatter together among the leaves" (I 410-414).

And with what gay abandon his peasants celebrate the arrival of spring (I 340-350)!—a passage imitated from the fifth book of Lucretius' *Of the Nature of Things* (1399-1402).

La Fontaine's animals, animated by the same "unfathomable joy," Virgil's "nescio qua dulcedine," sing the same hymn, dance the same dance in honor of Apollo or Ceres or Venus or the mere fact of being alive and in good spirits. There is Janot Lapin, who goes to pay homage to the rising sun amidst the thyme and the dew (VII 16); the well-nourished rat, who diverts himself on the banks of a marsh (IV 11); the heron, ambling along a crystal stream (VII 4); the swallow, joyfully skimming the sky and the water (X 6); the voluptuous oyster, palpitating in the sun and and the refreshing breezes (VIII 9). And there is La Fontaine himself and his hymn to Volupté. It is the same eternal doxology.

La Fontaine's hymn opens with a somewhat different theme:

O douce Volupté, sans qui, dès notre enfance,
Le vivre et le mourir nous deviendraient égaux;
Aimant universel de tous les animaux,
Que tu sais attirer avecque violence!
　　Par toi tout se meut ici-bas.
　　C'est pour toi, c'est pour tes appas,
　　Que nous courons après la peine:
　　Il n'est soldat, ni capitaine,
Ni ministre d'Etat, ni prince, ni sujet,
　　Qui ne t'ait pour unique objet.
Nous autres nourrissons, si pour fruit de nos veilles
Un bruit délicieux ne charmait nos oreilles,
Si nous ne nous sentions chatouillés de ce son,
　　Ferions-nous un mot de chanson?

Oh sweet Volupté, without whom, from our childhood,
Living and dying were equivalent to us;
Universal magnet of all animals,
How violently you know how to attract us!
　　Here below all is moved by you.
　　It is for you, it is for your attractions,
　　That we welcome difficulties:

No soldier, nor captain,
Nor minister of State, nor prince, nor subject,
But has you as his single object.
We other nurslings, if as the fruit of our wakes
A delicious noise did not charm our ears,
Were we not tickled by this sound,
Would we make a single word of song?

These introductory verses are more difficult than the concluding aria. We can understand what La Fontaine means when he
celebrates Volupté as the source of all animate existence. But
what is the Volupté that spurs soldiers, statesmen, princes, and
poets on to their exacting labors? And what is the "delicious
noise" that charms the poet's ear? The meaning becomes clearer
if we compare the passage with the corresponding passage in
Lucretius' invocation to Venus (I 21-28):

"Since you alone govern the nature of things and without you
nothing emerges on the sacred threshold of existence and nothing joyful or lovely may be created, I seek your partnership in
writing these verses which I am striving to compose about the
nature of things for our Memmius whom you, oh goddess, have
willed to excel in all things, illustrious forever. For his sake, therefore, goddess, give my words immortal charm."

La Fontaine has appropriated Lucretius' view of Venus as a
source not only of natural fecundation but of human inspira-
tion. The imperious power through which all lovely and joyful
things emerge "on the sacred threshold of existence" may work
more freely and more directly in the realm of natural existence.
Only when she is working through the agency of the human
imagination does Venus give "immortal charm" to her creations.
La Fontaine, unlike Lucretius, never requested Venus to make
his poetry immortal. Apparently (he was on fairly intimate terms
with this particular goddess) she did so of her own accord.

Chronological Table

		La Fontaine's Age
1621	La Fontaine is born at Château-Thierry	
1622	(Birth of Molière)	1
1628	(Death of Malherbe)	7
1639	(Birth of Racine)	18
1641	He enters a theological seminary in Paris	20
1642	He leaves the seminary, either voluntarily or by expulsion	21
1643	He returns to Château-Thierry	22
1645-1647	He studies law in Paris; is a member of a literary group which includes his future friends, the poets Maucroix and Pellisson	24-26
1647	He marries Marie Héricart and returns to Château-Thierry	26
1648	(Death of Voiture)	27
1652	He buys the office of forest warden at Château-Thierry	31
1653	Birth of his son, Charles	32
1654	*L'Eunuque*, a comedy imitated from Terence, is published	33
1657	The Duc de Bouillon acquires the duchy of Château-Thierry and starts to buy back the local offices; La Fontaine will not be completely reimbursed until 1671	36

La Fontaine's
Age

1658 La Fontaine's father dies; La Fontaine inherits his 37
father's offices and many debts; he presents
Adonis to Fouquet, the Surintendant des Finances

1659 Fouquet asks La Fontaine to celebrate his new 38
palace at Vaux-le-Vicomte in a poem

1659- Fouquet pays La Fontaine a quarterly pension; 38-40
1661 La Fontaine divides his time between Paris, Vaux,
and Château-Thierry; at Vaux he renews previous
friendship with Maucroix and Pellisson and becomes acquainted with many other literary figures
of the day; in Paris he meets Racine

1661 Arrest of Fouquet 40

1664- La Fontaine holds a position in the household of 43-51
1672 the dowager Duchesse d'Orléans in the Luxem-
bourg Palace, but lives with his uncle by marriage, Jannart, on the quai des Orfèvres; he meets
La Rochefoucauld, Madame de La Fayette, and
Madame de Sévigné; during this period he becomes separated from his wife, who returns to
Château-Thierry

1664 *Nouvelles en vers tirée(s) de Boccace et de l'Arioste* 43
par M. de L. F.

1665 *Contes et Nouvelles en vers de M. de La Fontaine* 44

1666 *Deuxième partie des Contes et Nouvelles en vers,* 45
de M. de La Fontaine

1668 *Fables choisies mises en vers par M. de La Fontaine* 47
(Books I-VI)

1669 *Les Amours de Psyché et de Cupidon, par M. de La* 48
Fontaine; a slightly revised version of *Adonis* is
published in the same volume

		La Fontaine's Age
1671	*Contes et Nouvelles en vers de M. de La Fontaine, troisième partie*	50
	Fables nouvelles et autres poésies de M. de La Fontaine; the eight previously unpublished fables will be republished in Books VII, VIII and IX of La Fontaine's collected fables.	
1672	Death of the Duchesse d'Orléans	51
1673	La Fontaine goes to live with Madame de La Sablière in the rue Neuve-des-Petits-Champs	52
	Poème de la Captivité de saint Malc par M. de La Fontaine	
	(Death of Molière)	
1674	La Fontaine begins *Daphné*, an opera requested and subsequently rejected by Lully	53
	(Boileau's *Art poétique*)	
	Nouveaux Contes de Monsieur de La Fontaine is published secretly	
1675	*Nouveaux Contes* is banned by the police	54
1678-1679	New edition of *Fables Choisies mises en vers* (augmented by Books VII and VIII, 1678, and Books IX, X and XI, 1679)	57-58
1680	(Death of Fouquet)	59
	Madame de La Sablière begins to devote herself to religious and charitable works; shortly afterwards she moves to the rue Saint-Honoré, lodging La Fontaine in another house next door	
1682	*Poème du Quinquina et autres ouvrages en vers de M. de La Fontaine*; the volume contains two new contes, the pastoral opera *Galatée*, and the unfinished *Daphné*	61
1683	*Le Rendez-vous*, a comedy since lost, is presented at the Comédie Française; it is performed only four times	62

La Fontaine's
Age

1684   La Fontaine is admitted to the Académie Française;   63
       he reads the *Discours à Madame de La Sablière*
       at his first session

1687   A *Monseigneur l'Evêque de Soissons, en lui don-*   66
       nant un Quintilien

1688   Madame de La Sablière goes to live in the hospital   67
       for incurables

1691   *Astrée, tragédie lyrique*, imitated from d'Urfé's   70
       novel, is presented at the Opéra; it is performed
       only six times

1693   Madame de La Sablière dies; La Fontaine goes to   72
       live with his friend d'Hervart
       La Fontaine is converted to Christianity by the
       Abbé Poujet; he makes a public condemnation
       of his contes and burns a new comedy

1694   *Fables Choisies, par M. de La Fontaine* (Book XII   73
       of La Fontaine's collected fables)

1695   La Fontaine dies in the house of d'Hervart   74

1699   (Death of Racine)

Index

Abstemius, 92

Aesop, 4, 5, 6, 7, 15, 23, 24, 26, 28, 65, 66, 83, 102, 126, 131, 137

Alain (Emile Chartier), 109, 136

Anne of Austria, 74

Ariosto, Ludovico, 17

Aristoteles, 150

Auden, Wystan Hugh, 44

Augustine, 147

Austen, Jane, 85; *Pride and Prejudice*, 88

Balzac, Honoré de, 85

Baudelaire, Charles, 158

Bernier, François, 143; *Abrégé de la philosophie de Gassendi*, 143, 146, 149

Boase, Alan, 45

Boccaccio, Giovanni, 17

Boileau-Despréaux, Nicolas, 47, 81, 177; *L'Art poétique*, 16, 19, 37, 69; *Le Bûcheron et la Mort*, 132-133

Bossuet, Jacques-Bénigne, 91, 104

Bouillon, Duchesse de, 4, 164-165

Bourgogne, Duc de, 55, 119

Brossette, Claude, 81

Bruno, Giordano, 150; *Dialogue on the Infinite*, 150

Brunot, Ferdinand, 35

Caligula, 92

Camus, Albert, 109

Carroll, Lewis, 31

Chaucer, Geoffrey, 85; *The Miller's Tale*, 88; *The Nun's Priest's Tale*, 85

Chénier, André, 31

Chopin, Frédéric, 58

Claudel, Paul, 36, 46, 136, 137

Clutton-Brock, Arthur, 108

Coleridge, Samuel Taylor, 11, 31; *The Rime of the Ancient Mariner*, 121

Colletet, Claudine, 116, 117

Concini, Concino, 80, 87

Corneille, Pierre, 46, 53; *Andromède*, 43

Corrozet, Gilles, 31

Coppée, François, 63

Cyrano de Bergerac, 111

Democritus, 147

Descartes, René, 19, 84, 141-147, 150, 152

Desportes, Philippe, 39, 70
Dickens, Charles, 85; *Martin Chuzzlewit*, 102
Donne, John, *The Canonization*, 158, 163

Eliot, Thomas Stearns, 27-28, 30, 44, 81, 121, 166; *The Hollow Men*, 165; *The Love Song of J. Alfred Prufrock*, 49, 50; *Preludes*, 49
Enghien, Duc d', 138
Epicurus, 147, 177, 178
Euripides, *Medea*, 65

Fables, see La Fontaine
Fontenelle, Bernard de, 19
Fouquet, Nicolas, 17, 19, 20, 63, 64, 91, 127
Francis I, 86
Frost, Robert, *After Apple Picking*, 49

Galileo, 150
Gassendi, Pierre, 142, 143, 147, 149, 150
Giraudoux, Jean, 46
Gohin, Ferdinand, 39, 52, 57

Handford, S. A., 4
Haudent, Guillaume, 31
Henry IV, 81, 90, 92, 94
Hobbes, Thomas, 119
Homer, 16, 23, 24, 25, 28, 180; *The Iliad*, 70, 71
Horace, 64, 135, 165, 166, 171, 174, 175, 183; *Satires*, 32-33
Hugo, Victor, 39, 43
Huret, Jules, 44

James, Henry, 96
Jasinski, René, 143

Keats, John, *Endymion*, 98

Lafayette, Madame de, 4, 18
La Fontaine, Jean de:
  Adonis, 17, 21, 47-48, 50, 52, 63, 70, 72, 73-74, 77, 78, 91, 155
  Les Amours de Psyché et de Cupidon, 17, 21, 65, 79, 146, 153, 154, 160, 175-176, 177, 178, 185-186
  La Captivité de Saint Malc, 17
  Clymène, 63-64, 66, 76, 89, 171
  Contes, 17-18, 32, 128
  Discours à Madame de La Sablière, 143, 176, 177
  Epître à Huet, Evêque de Soissons, 32, 80-81, 104, 171
  Fables: Preface 23-24, 179; A Monseigneur le Dauphin, 23; L'aigle et l'escarbot (II 8), 78; L'aigle et le hibou (V 18), 93; L'aigle, la laie, et la chatte (III 6), 94-96; L'aigle et la pie (XII 11), 35, 134-135; L'alouette et ses petits, avec le maître d'un champs (IV 22), 40, 56, 129, 165, 183-184; L'âne vêtu de la peau du lion (V 21), 107; Un animal dans la lune (VII 18), 126; Les animaux malades de la peste (VII 1), 101-104, 180-181; L'araignée et l'hirondelle (X 6), 105-106, 130, 182-183, 185; Le chat,

la belette, et le petit lapin (VII 16), 40, 107, 130, 185; Le chat et le rat (VIII 22), 128; Le chat et un vieux rat (III 18), 128; La chauve-souris et les deux belettes (II 5), 108-109; Le chêne et le roseau (I 22), 82-83, 133, 166; Le cheval et le loup (V 8), 32; La colombe et la fourmi (II 12), 41; Le combat des rats et des belettes (IV 6), 73, 74; Les compagnons d'Ulysse (XII 1), 55, 119; Contre ceux qui ont le goût difficile (II 1), 15, 65-70, 73, 91, 138-139; Le corbeau et le renard (I 2), 2-11, 97, 138; Le corbeau voulant imiter l'aigle (II 16), 107; La cour du lion (VII 7), 90-91, 92; Le curé et le mort (VII 11), 106; Démocrite et les Abdéritains (VIII 26), 105; Le dépositaire infidèle (IX 1), 28; Les deux aventuriers et le talisman (X 13), 35; Les deux coqs (VII 13), 74, 181-182; Les deux pigeons (IX 2), 53-54, 155-167; Les deux rats, le renard, et l'oeuf (IX 21), 143, 147-150, 151, 152, 184; La Discorde (VI 20), 38; Discours à Madame de La Sablière (IX 20), 143, 144-147, 148, 150; L'éléphant et le singe de Jupiter (XII 21), 72, 107, 118; L'enfouisseur et son compère (X 4), 36; Epilogue (XI), 29, 139-140, 153;

Le fermier, le chien, et le renard (XI 3), 73; La fille (VII 5), 135; Le geai paré des plumes du paon (IV 9), 107; La génisse, la chèvre, et la brebis en société avec le lion (I 6), 100; Le gland et la citrouille (IX 4), 111-112, 118; La goutte et l'araignée (III 8), 36; La grenouille qui se veut faire aussi grosse que le boeuf (I 3), 107; La grenouille et le rat (IV 11), 31, 34, 137, 185; Le héron (VII 4), 25-26, 27, 33, 58, 138, 185; L'homme et la couleuvre (X 1), 35, 119-121; L'homme qui court après la Fortune et l'homme qui l'attend dans son lit (VII 12), 57-58, 160; L'huître et les plaideurs (IX 9), 107; La jeune veuve (VI 21), 41; La laitière et le pot au lait (VII 10), 56, 106, 115-116, 126, 166-167; Le lièvre et les grenouilles (II 14), 39-40; Le lièvre et la tortue (VI 10), 51, 129; Le lion amoureux (IV 1), 160; Le lion devenu vieux (III 14), 96; Le lion et le moucheron (II 9), 80, 87; La lionne et l'ours (X 12), 77-78; Le loup et l'agneau (I 10), 33, 39, 99-100; Le loup et les bergers (X 5), 114-115, 119; Le loup et le chien maigre (IX 10), 106, 113-114; Le loup devenu berger (III 3), 112-113; Le loup, la mère, et l'enfant

(IV 16), 113, 128; Le loup plaidant contre le renard par devant le singe (II 3), 107, 134; Le loup et le renard (XI 6), 87, 97-99, 166; Le mal marié (VII 2), 53-54, 135, 137; Le marchand, le gentilhomme, le pâtre, et le fils du roi (X 15), 38; Le meunier, son fils, et l'âne (III 1), 34, 40-41, 52-53, 58, 138; La Mort et le bûcheron (I 16), 131-132, 173; La Mort et le mourant (VIII 1), 173; La mouche et la fourmi (IV 3), 35; Les obsèques de la lionne (VIII 14), 84, 91-92; L'oracle et l'impie (IV 19), 41; L'ours et les deux compagnons (V 20), 106; Le petit poisson et le pêcheur (V 3), 38, 137; Le philosophe scythe (XII 20), 174, 177; Les poissons et le cormoran (X 3), 74; Le pot de terre et le pot de fer (V 2), 129; La querelle des chiens et des chats, et celle des chats et des souris (XII 8), 107; Le rat et l'éléphant (VIII 15), 27, 55, 107-108; Le rat et l'huître (VIII 9), 56-57, 75-76, 185; Le rat qui s'est retiré du monde (VII 3), 35; Le rat de ville et le rat des champs (I 9), 32-33; Le renard ayant la queue coupée (V 5), 39; Le renard et le bouc (III 5), 138; Le renard, le loup, et le cheval (XII 17), 32; Le renard et les poulets d'Inde (XII 18), 130; Rien de trop (IX 11), 118; Le rieur et les poissons (VIII 8), 59; Le savetier et le financier (VIII 2), 38; Le songe d'un habitant du Mogol (XI 4), 167, 174; Les souris et le chat-huant (XI 9), 143-144; Du thésauriseur et du singe (XII 3), 37; Le trésor et les deux hommes (IX 16), 103, 106; Tribut envoyé par les animaux à Alexandre (IV 12), 75; Les vautours et les pigeons (VII 8), 69; La vieille et les deux servantes (V 6), 79

Les filles de Minos, 177
Le Florentin, 116-117
Galatée, 53
Le Songe de Vaux, 17, 21, 63, 65, 76, 78, 127, 138, 151-152, 154
Letters, 20, 82, 163, 164-165, 172

Laforgue, Jules, 81, 165, 166
Lamartine, Alphonse de, 31
Lambert, Michel, 53
La Rochefoucauld, Duc de, 4, 18, 21, 119
La Sablière, Madame de, 21, 141, 143, 176
Lessing, Gotthold Ephraïm, 128
Locke, John, 105-106
Lorenz, Karl, 86, 114
Louis XIII, 86, 90
Louis XIV, 19, 86, 87, 91, 100-101, 105

Louis (the Dauphin), 23
Lovejoy, Arthur O., 163
Lucretius, 16, 147, 174, 175, 182; *Of the Nature of Things*, 22-23, 142, 149, 150, 172, 173, 178, 179, 181, 183, 184, 186
Lully, Jean-Baptiste, 116-117

Machiavelli, Niccolò, 88, 104
Maecenas, 174, 179
Malherbe, François de, 30, 34, 38, 39, 42, 45, 46, 47, 63, 64, 70, 74, 80, 81, 86, 87, 89, 91-92, 94, 104, 171, 177
Mallarmé, Stéphane, 44, 47
Marie-Thérèse, 91
Marlowe, Christopher, *Dr. Faustus*, 125
Marvell, Andrew, 166
Maucroix, François, 20
Memmius, 186
Milton, John, 53; *Lycidas*, 49, 60
Molé, Matthieu, 118
Molière (Jean-Baptiste Poquelin), 18, 21, 49, 126; *Les Fâcheux*, 21; *Le Misanthrope*, 8-9, 64, 165
Montaigne, Michel de, 21; *Apologie de Raimond Sebond*, 117-118, 119, 142, 143, 144, 147, 180
Mozart, Wolfgang Amédée, *The Marriage of Figaro*, 54

Ovid, *Metamorphoses*, 17, 70, 71

Pascal, Blaise, 21, 150, 172-173
Patru, Olivier, 16
Péguy, Charles, 109
Phaedrus, 6, 8, 15, 22, 23, 33, 65, 94

Pilpay, 120
Pintrel, Pierre, 115
Plato, 177-178; *The Republic*, 23-24, 25; *Timaeus*, 163
Proust, Marcel, 85, 137

Quennel, Peter, 18
Quinault, Philippe, 116-117

Rabelais, François, 5
Racan, Honoré de, 171
Racine, Jean, 18, 21, 30, 31, 46, 48, 50, 56, 126; *Andromaque*, 95
Régnier, Mathurin, 32, 127
Roman de Renart, Le, 85, 125
Rimbaud, Arthur, 63
Ronsard, Pierre, 19, 45, 80
Rossetti, Christina, *Eve*, 35
Rousseau, Jean-Jacques, 9, 105

Saint-Amant, 126, 127, 167
Saint-Evremond, Charles de, 4, 163, 172
Saint-Simon, Duc de, 91
Sarasin, Jean-François, 49
Scarron, Paul, *Virgile travesty*, 74
Seneca, *Epistles*, 115
Seton, Ernest, 104
Sévigné, Madame de, 4, 126-127
Shakespeare, William, 33, 37, 50, 112
Socrates, 23-24
Spinoza, Baruch, 110

Taine, Hippolyte, 84, 91
Theocritus, *Idyls*, 92
Théophile (Théophile de Viau), 118, 126, 127, 167, 181
Thucydides, 181
Trollope, Anthony, 85

Valéry, Paul, 47, 48, 155
Vinci, Leonardo da, 150
Virgil, 47, 48, 83; *Aeneid*, 16, 23, 67-69, 70, 73, 74, 75, 82, 115, 180, 183; *Eclogues*, 17, 92; *Georgics*, 23, 74, 82, 149-150, 167, 174, 175, 179-185

Voiture, Vincent, 31, 49, 63, 64, 89, 138

Wadsworth, Philip, 64
Wordsworth, William, 31

Yeats, William Butler, 130

In this volume, one of the authors of *An Age of Fiction* has turned to a consideration of the French fabulist La Fontaine. His fables belong to that rare category of poetry, a popular and familiar art which is also recognized as "great." And yet, perhaps because of their very familiarity, the fundamental character and direction of the fables as poetry are not very widely understood. Mrs. Guiton's approach is suggested by La Fontaine's ultimate claim:

> Thus my muse, by a limpid stream,
>   Translated into the language of the
>   gods
>   Everything said under the skies
> By so many beings borrowing the voice
>   of nature.

Working toward La Fontaine's own definition of his fable poetry, the author proceeds to show how La Fontaine, using the humble and traditionally prosaic fable form, escaped or revitalized the established conventions and attitudes of late seventeenth-century poetry in France: how he gradually perfected a new instrument adapted to his own end of translating the "voice of nature" into "the language of the gods," or poetry.

Depending primarily on the internal evidence of the fables themselves, Mrs. Guiton examines the language, the sound patterns, the rhythms which bring the fable metaphor to life as an imagery of movement, gesture, attitude. And she shows how the reactivated fable metaphor, in all its humor and grace and vitality, expresses La Fontaine's personal conception of the natural universe, this universe including man. Her book is written for the general reader and requires no special knowledge of the French language nor of French literature. "A poet so